Pye

Tales from the Front Line

LUKE FLETCHER

Tales from the Front Line

pitch

First published by Pitch Publishing, 2020

Pitch Publishing
A2 Yeoman Gate
Yeoman Way
Worthing
Sussex
BN13 3QZ
www.pitchpublishing.co.uk
info@pitchpublishing.co.uk

A CIP catalogue record is available for this book from the British Library.

ISBN 978 1 78531 687 6

Typesetting and origination by Pitch Publishing

Printed and bound by TJ Books, Padstow, UK

Contents

Foreword by Freddie Flintoff

I APPRECIATE being asked to write a few words for Fletch because he is genuinely one of my favourite cricketers.

The first time I spoke to him was when he was a young lad doing a 12th man stint for England a few years back.

You get wrapped up in your own bubble on those occasions but in him I saw somebody that was a lad after my own heart.

I could tell he was whole-hearted, loved his cricket and would be fun to be around.

Every team needs a character, someone who will make you laugh and will lift the dressing room when it's feeling a bit down.

When I played, Darren Gough filled that role and I see Fletch as being someone in the same mould.

It's easy just to see the fun side of things though because Fletch is someone who is not just a character, he's also a very good bowler who doesn't get the credit he deserves.

I remember watching him bowl for Notts at Liverpool one year and thinking, 'This guy's brilliant.'

He's a bit of an old-school bowler but I've watched him many times on television and been impressed, he's got a yorker on tap, one or two other varieties and is the type of character to define a team.

Modern sport can be so sterile, so it's refreshing to see someone like Fletch who gives the impression that every day he's playing for Nottinghamshire is the best day of his life.

I understand what his teammates see in him and why he has such a large following of fans. It's because his enthusiasm is infectious.

Hopefully he has a few more years left in the tank but when he does finish playing he'll look back on his career with such pride at what he's done.

Some of the best days of my life were at Lancashire and I know he'll also look back and say, 'How good was that?'

Introduction

HELLO. THE odds are that you've never heard of me before and have picked this book up by mistake.

If that is the case, then I'd better introduce myself. I'm just a fairly normal bloke from Nottingham who has been extremely lucky in life.

Born into a loving, working-class family, I've been incredibly fortunate to spend more than a decade in professional sport.

As you will see, things could have been very different for me. I was never the brightest academically and I certainly had no plans to waste my life in a boring 9–5 office job.

Hard graft was never going to be an issue and I certainly had no qualms about working in a fast food restaurant until fate lent a hand and gave me an opportunity to play cricket for a living.

Even more importantly, to me at least, I've been able to do it while representing my own little corner of the world.

From the very first time that I pulled on a Nottinghamshire sweater I have been proud to wear the colours and represent them. I'd also like to think folks would agree that I've given everything I could to help them be successful.

There have been occasions, of course, where it's not gone as well as I would have liked but – hey-ho, that's sport, I suppose.

I should tell you at this point that I'm quite a big lad, comfortably qualifying for the 'gentle giant' category at 6ft 6in tall and weighing 100kg (on a good day!).

While that hardly fits the stereotype of a modern-day athlete, I'm reminded of a quote from the legendary former Yorkshire and England fast bowler Fred Trueman:

'To be a fast bowler you need a big heart and a big backside.'

That's that box ticked then!

While I've often had the knack of being in the wrong place at the wrong time, I try and live life with a smile on my face and usually manage to have a laugh and a joke about it, often at my own expense.

And I should also point out that not all of the stories you will read here paint me in a good light. There have been times when I know I've perhaps crossed the line and had a fair amount of making up to do.

Still, it's all part of life's rich pattern.

I'd rarely considered that my tales might one day warrant being put on to pages for others to enjoy but the coronavirus epidemic that swept the world halted so many things, including professional sport.

People, including me, needed a focus in their lives, so it has been nice to reminisce and recall a few favourite moments.

I hope you all enjoy *Tales From The Front Line*.

1

In The Beginning

AS BEFITS a finely tuned athlete, I made my entry into the world just as the opening ceremony of the 1988 Seoul Olympics was concluding.

Alan and Jane Fletcher's new arrival was a big lad, nudging 9lb at birth. 'He was almost a tenner,' my dad kept repeating as his mates took him out to wet the baby's head.

The number one record in the charts that week was 'He Ain't Heavy, He's My Brother', something appropriate for my elder sibling to utter.

Tom is two years older than me, and Mum and Dad kept things at regular intervals because a third son, Sam, followed a further two years after I arrived.

Dad worked as a coal miner at Annesley Colliery, disappearing underground to graft in some of the toughest conditions known to man.

His shift work and long hours of absence left Mum with the challenge of rearing three permanently hungry lads.

My earliest memories were always of the three of us playing together, either in the garden or on the street. Our neighbourhood seemingly had lots of youngsters all around the same age, all sharing the same hobbies and interests and all getting into the usual scrapes that kids of that age seem to attract.

It was usually football that kept us occupied, playing matches between ourselves until it was time for tea. The summer months were taken up with the occasional game of cricket, apart from the really hot days when we'd have massive water-fights. The Fletcher boys were usually more than a match for anyone that dared to take us on.

Football began to take over my life. I regularly played in goal and joined my local side, Bulwell Rangers, at an early age, playing matches at weekends, with one evening a week set aside for training.

Cantrell Primary, a five-minute walk away, was my first school and I really enjoyed my time there, particularly as there was always lots of sport to play – either organised or among ourselves.

Ralph Surman was one of my early teachers and we still keep in touch now.

* * *

Ralph Surman: 'Luke started in my vertically grouped infant class of 1992–93. The class contained those reaching their sixth and seventh birthdays, in a mixed ability setting.

'He was larger than his contemporaries and could be mistaken for a Year Two child when you saw them all together.

'Luke was very popular and was well liked by all the other children. He was very calm and relaxed and undertook schoolwork at his own pace.

'He learnt to read very quickly and was competent in basic maths. I wouldn't say he was enthusiastic to undertake written tasks but was more than capable. One feature was always the great support he received from his parents with his studies. They were lovely.

'Our school concert in 1993 was based on Elvis Presley, and I always remember Luke playing "My Teddy Bear". He wore pyjamas and carried his own teddy bear under his arm while dancing to the classic Elvis number.'

* * *

I also had a teacher called Mr Osborne and during my time with him I was given a very strong life lesson. He believed in rewarding his pupils whenever they did something well, so had a pack of strawberry bon-bons on a shelf.

The teacher would dish one out to anyone who'd done outstanding work in his classroom. I liked strawberry bon-bons but there was a pretty slim chance of me earning one the conventional way.

One breaktime I hung around in the classroom until everyone else had gone out to play and climbed on a chair to reach them.

I was just helping myself to a load of the tasty confectionery when Mr Osborne walked back in.

Oh s**t. Caught in the act. Bang to rights.

Feeling sure I'd be given lines, a detention or maybe even the ruler, I was a little bemused that I seemed to have dodged any form of capital punishment.

But Mr Osborne was crafty.

What's the worst way a kid can be punished?

He waited until my mum and dad came to pick me up and told them what I'd been up to. Grassed up, good and proper!

The next day was a Saturday and my dad took me down the road, at the back of our house, to Bulwell Police Station, which was only a five-minute walk away.

A policeman took me from my dad and put me in a cell.

Genuinely.

I was six years old and petrified.

Nowadays, I'm sure a cocky youngster would demand to know his or her rights and refuse to speak until their solicitor was present.

That wasn't for me. Even if I'd been a bit more worldly-wise I knew this wasn't a time for showboating.

The policeman gave me a strict talking-to about stealing and what would happen to me if I did it again. A life behind bars and more porridge than Goldilocks seemed to be my fate if I ventured near to the strawberry bon-bons again.

He frightened the life out of me and the floodgates opened. I began to sob, then I cried, then I screamed the place down.

'I'm soooooooorrrrryyyy,' I wailed.

I was really upset, so upset that my dad obviously felt a little guilty about what I'd been put through and he took me to the sweet shop and bought me a choccy bar afterwards.

Years later he told me that it had all been set up. He'd popped into the police station and asked if someone could have a word with me but even he didn't think they'd go to the extremes of putting me in a cell and scaring the life out of me.

Not funny, Dad. Not funny.

His reasons for doing it were sound enough, though. He didn't want anything else to go missing at school and me get the blame for it, he didn't want me to have a reputation and he didn't want me to be known as a thief, so thought he'd nip it in the bud early.

There was one other time that my dad taught me a lesson for not doing as I was told.

The five of us were in Majorca on holiday – I would be about ten or 11. The beach was absolutely rammed full of tourists, hardly a spare space to be found.

Tom and Sam were doing their own thing but I wanted to go down to the sea and pestered my parents until I got my own way.

'All right, go and play but stay in this section here,' they said.

It wasn't long before my attention span wandered. I could see a speedboat moored up a little way along from where I was. Although the more I paddled towards it, the further away it seemed to be getting.

The boat was probably 200 or 300 yards away from my original starting point but it seemed as if I'd wandered even further and when I looked back I got quite a shock – I didn't know where I was. Still, I was having a good time.

I'd probably been gone for about 40 minutes or so when a helicopter started doing low runs over the beach. They were clearly looking for something ... or someone!

Wandering back through the crowds of people, I bumped into my dad, who had formed his own one-man search party for me. He gave me a right roasting for going off like that and told me that I'd been reported missing and that the helicopter had been sent up to search for me.

Naturally, I believed him and felt awful and didn't leave my parents' side for the rest of the holiday.

I felt guilty at having put so many people to so much trouble. Emergency services have better things to do than search a crowded beach for a little boy who can't do as he's told.

That guilt stayed with me, into my teens, into my 20s and almost into my 30s, when it cropped up in conversation again and Dad confessed that he hadn't reported me missing at all!

You may be surprised to hear that, even in primary school, I was a big lad and so was easily spotted in all my early school and team photographs. When we were able to play sport I liked to go in goal for the football and chose to keep wicket on the rare occasions we played cricket.

In the photos I was usually thrust in the centre of the back row, towering over my mates.

I loved running about and playing sport and couldn't wait for breaktimes or for school to be over so we could start up our matches again.

Every day Mum gave us a couple of quid for our dinner but I would always be up to no good and used to gamble it before school started.

We used to play a game called 'Wally' (pronounced Wall-E) and sometimes I'd be on a hot streak and have about 12 quid in my pocket.

The game involved standing about two metres from a wall and throwing a coin at it; closest to the wall took the cash.

It was usually 50p a go and I became good enough to hustle at it, getting to know the surfaces pretty well and working a system to ensure I'd be the winner.

More often than not it worked out well for me but on other days I'd lose badly and have nothing left. Desperate times call for desperate measures but I'd thought this through because Mum was a school dinner lady.

I would go and see her and make out I was still hungry and scrounge a couple of cream buns or something for lunch. I did that for about five years; it was great. All the other ladies in the kitchen knew me as well and they'd spoil me, slipping me slices of pizza or whatever was on the menu that day.

Perhaps that's the reason I'm such a big lad now!

Football was everything at that time. Morning, noon and night,I would play as often as I could. Big for my age, I was a natural to go in goal but I also enjoyed playing outfield as well and managed to have a little bit of success in both positions.

My senior year at Cantrell Primary coincided with the school entering the football team in a nationwide competition, the Adidas Predator Cup.

This was a fairly drawn-out event, lasting many local district rounds, before becoming regional and then national.

Somehow, we kept winning.

It was a seven-a-side tournament on a pitch that was around three-quarters of the size of a full one. Our progress through the rounds made us more and more excitable and suddenly there were huge opportunities ahead of us.

We qualified for the county finals, to be played at Nottingham Forest's City Ground. The match should have been played on a Monday – maybe during a half-term holiday, I'm not sure. But I couldn't wait. I was so much looking forward to it but then, disaster struck.

Over the weekend I was larking around on a high wall and fell off.

I badly hurt my knee and that was that, I had to miss out and my City Ground experience was limited to just cheering the rest of the lads on.

Without my cat-like reflexes, Cantrell Primary had to make alternative arrangements. A lad by the name of Paddy Gamble was put in goal. I don't recall if I gave him any tips or not but I'd like to think I was instrumental in setting him on his way towards a career that eventually saw him on the books of Nottingham Forest, Mansfield Town and several successful non-league sides.

Paddy had a blinder and was a hero as we won on penalties. The opposition were Fernwood Primary from Wollaton and the decisive moment came when a lad called Eddie Somekh slammed his spot kick against the crossbar. I didn't know him at the time but a few years later Eddie and I became good mates and played a fair amount of cricket together for Papplewick and Linby CC. Needless to say his penalty miss rarely got mentioned!

Although I'd only been cheering from the sidelines as we won at the City Ground, I was more than happy to join in the celebrations and look forward to the regional heats that followed.

We had to go to Retford, to play a team from Sheffield or Barnsley. The precise details aren't important; what you really need to know is the part I played in getting the win that took us through to the finals.

The coaching staff had decided to stick with Paddy in goal but brought me into the side as a deep-lying, ball-winning central defender with the licence to pop forward and show off.

Immediately we went a goal behind and the omens weren't good. We were still trailing deep into the contest when I had a foray forward and bundled home a loose ball to make it all square.

Another penalty shoot-out seemed likely as we approached the final seconds. I was on the halfway line when the ball dropped to me. Instinctively I took it on the volley and gave it a mighty left-footed thump and could scarcely believe my luck as it flew over the goalkeeper and into the top corner.

What a screamer!

Pandemonium followed as my teammates swallowed me up in sheer disbelief. One or two of them were wide-eyed and wearing expressions that I have become used to in later life whenever Samit Patel is confronted by a dessert trolley.

Our victory meant that we were through to the finals and they would be staged at Old Trafford before a Manchester United home match. It's fair to say that we were pretty chuffed by this turn of events.

We travelled up the night before and stayed in a hotel, with our parents joining us on the day.

Now how do you reward your semi-final hero, the guy who popped up with two goals to hand the school their most prestigious day of all time?

You drop him. Yep, that's right, they told me I was to be sub. Some lad, whose folks were very influential and in with the teachers, was named in my place. He was a Manchester United supporter and I think they thought he deserved it more.

So, I was somewhat sour-faced and miserable when I took my place on the bench for the first half. We went 1-0 down and I was brought on as an outfield player at half-time but there was no more magic left in the tank and the score remained the same.

The main event on that April 2000 afternoon was Manchester United against Sunderland, a match that featured a couple of goals from Ole Gunnar Solksjaer as the home team won 4-0.

I remember we had seats – good seats – right at the top of the stand and it seemed to take forever to walk all the way up there.

When Beckham, Neville, Scholes and co. popped off for their half-time oranges we went back on to the pitch to be presented with our medals and to do a lap of honour.

Heady stuff for a group of young lads from Cantrell Primary. Funnily enough we have all remained in touch since leaving school and have our own WhatsApp group these days, 'The Class of 2000'.

While most of the lads were pretty down in the dumps, I was surprisingly chipper. That's because I had another treat lined up, just around the corner.

My goalkeeping performances for Bulwell had got me noticed and I'd had a representative call-up for the Nottingham City Boys.

They had also entered a nationwide competition and made good progress. Such good progress, in fact, that we had qualified for the finals, which were to be held at Wembley Stadium.

As with my goals for Cantrell Primary, I stepped up when it mattered by saving three out of five penalty kicks in the match that got us through to the finals.

Once more we had another brilliant day but lost 1-0, with former England goalkeeper Peter Shilton presenting us with our medals.

We then settled down to watch an England versus Scotland match from the stands but I can't remember whether it was a schoolboy or university international.

Up until this point I'd had a bit of a playground soft spot for Liverpool, yet bizarrely the first shirt I owned was a white Spurs one, with the badge on. I'm not sure where it came from; it was possibly even a hand-me-down.

That all changed once Dad started taking me to the City Ground to see Nottingham Forest play.

David Platt had taken over as manager and I absolutely loved everything about the experience, particularly the noise and the passion of the fans.

We didn't go all that often but Forest had become my team and I started to follow their fortunes closely.

Our exploits in those two competitions had drawn a bit of attention from the scouts and I was invited to go for trials at Forest, Leeds United and Notts County.

Purely because a lot of my mates played there I chose Notts County but it turned out to be a terrible decision and I regret it to this day.

I carried on going until they released me when I was aged 13 or 14, citing in my final report, 'Luke is a good shot-stopper but lacks agility' – at least they managed to pick up on that fairly early!

2

Having A Hoot

IT WAS quite a long time before cricket came on my radar. Our street matches were usually played with either a tennis ball or a rubber ball but I'll never forget the first time I played with a proper hard ball. I'd had no guidance and popped on a pair of batting gloves when it was my turn to have a knock. Unbeknown to me at the time, there is a difference between right-handers' gloves and left-handers'.

I had incorrectly popped on some lefties and went out to bat on this absolute dog of a wicket. Typically, the first ball reared up off the uneven surface and whacked me fully on my unprotected right thumb, making it throb like something out of a *Tom and Jerry* cartoon.

Apart from those street matches the only other time I'd play would be on our annual summer outing to Skegness, where we'd have a bit of a hit on the beach.

My first trip to Trent Bridge did nothing to foster a lasting love for the game. When I was about ten we went there on a midweek school trip, with Mr Surman and Mr Marston the teachers in charge.

I reckon it was for a Notts v Middlesex match and they stuck us all together in the William Clarke Stand. We were a noisy chattering bunch who paid very little attention to what was happening in the middle.

It was utterly boring. The most exciting thing for me was being able to see the City Ground floodlights. Apart from that I just spent the time scoffing my packed lunch and fooling around as usual. When the time came to leave they gave us all some gifts, an orange wind ball, a pencil and a rubber.

My secondary education was spent at Henry Mellish Grammar School, a fountain of knowledge that no longer exists, having been replaced in recent years by one of those fancy academies.

Online, should you wish, you can still look up all the noteworthy people that attended Henry Mellish over the years. According to them, their famous former alumni are:

Sir Neil Cossons OBE

Dr Sidney Holgate CBE

Professor Peter J. Taylor

Sir David Greenaway

Archdeacon Garth Norman

And Luke Fletcher, a cricketer.

I don't recall being in the same lessons as any of those other noble gentlemen but I'm honoured to make the list, nonetheless.

By all accounts it was a really posh school back in the day but when I went it was in what they called 'special measures' so perhaps it wasn't surprising that they knocked it down.

There were always one or two rascals at the school and I've heard that Robin Hood himself was there, a year or two ahead of me. Apparently, he was a fairly decent bloke, taking from the rich and giving to the poor!

Academically, I was neither a front-runner nor a bottom-of-the-classer, leaving school with ten GSCE qualifications. One of those was down to a teacher called Graham Roberts, who I still see regularly at Trent Bridge.

* * *

Graham Roberts: 'I first came across Luke in a Year Seven maths class when he was aged 11. Even then it was a squeeze for him to sit behind a desk! I'd already taught his brother, Tom, who was really quiet so it was quite a surprise to see what a contrast Luke was.

'Right from the outset the only thing that really motivated him was sport. Luke was much taller than the other lads in his year group and was a budding goalkeeper in the soccer team. In fact, he was the only goalkeeper we ever had who regularly asked if he could go up for every corner as he was so tall and powerful. He also used to take all the free kicks in his own half and tried to score directly – with occasional success.

'Ironically at this time (and to our shame!) the school didn't play a great deal of cricket so we didn't see the best of Fletch. I do remember a colleague from a neighbouring school relating a story of when Henry Mellish turned up to play them at indoor cricket in a small gymnasium. Fletch smacked every ball that was bowled at him for six!!

'The rest of his time at school was spent playing sport as often as possible and doing as little as possible at everything else.

'His technology teacher told me that Luke came to him one day and asked if he would isolate him from another teacher's lesson because it was so boring (he had a very low boredom threshold). The teacher said no but found out that Fletch had gone into the lesson and promptly fallen asleep!

'I came across Luke more when he was in Year Ten, aged 14, as he was in my GCSE maths group. That was a battle!

'The aim was to get all of the students a pass at grade C or above. This was always going to be a challenge, especially when Luke found out that I played cricket.

'In the middle of a lesson he would often try and divert me from the work that he was supposed to be doing to get me engaged in a cricket discussion. I remember vividly a conversation, that must have lasted half an hour, about how to set a field for a leg-spin bowler!

'At that time we ran table tennis sessions, both at lunchtime and after school and Luke was a keen participant. I regularly played games against him and always came out on top but he had a keenness to get better and that led to him having to serve a detention with me.

'At the end of one particular maths session it was lunchtime and I had told everyone to pack away their things and wait for the bell. While chatting with some other students I realised that Luke wasn't there.

'"Where's Fletch?" I asked but realised that he had shot off to ensure he had got a table to play on.

'I promptly phoned down to a colleague who intercepted him and sent him back, much to his annoyance.

'His "punishment" was to spend the entire lunch period with me. I can't remember what I made him do but it probably ended with a cricket discussion!

'Towards the end of Year 11 we took a group of Luke's peers to a hotel in Matlock Bath for a focussed period of revision before the exams. Luke battled away during the day but clearly ensured he enjoyed himself in the evenings. I lost count of the number of times we walked down the corridor after lights out to hear Luke's voice above all the others.

'At the last parents' evening before Luke left school I can recall sitting with him and his mum and saying what a great lad he was but that he wasn't going to do himself justice in the exam unless he really knuckled down.

'I remember saying to him that he couldn't rely on making it as a cricketer as it was really difficult to make a career of it!

'How those words have come back to haunt me. I often meet Luke's mum at Trent Bridge and remember that conversation.

'The upshot of all of this was that Luke got his higher grade pass in maths and it must rank as one of the highlights of my teaching career!'

* * *

When my time came to step out into the big wide world I didn't have a clue what I wanted to do, so opted for college, studying sports science at the Adams Building in Hockley.

It wasn't what I'd expected really, being all about massage therapy and physiotherapy, that sort of thing.

I quickly realised it wasn't for me and got out of there as fast as I could but only went as far as doing something similar at South Notts College.

My options had been limited but the only way I could claim any funding was to keep turning up and making sure my name was ticked on the register.

It was something called the EMA grant and was worth between £50 and £70 per week, enough for me to give my mum a bit of board and have a few quid left over to go out with.

Being stuck behind a desk was never going to keep me motivated for very long and I yearned to get out into the big wide world and start doing something with my life, so I continued to look for other options.

Brother Tom had become a bus driver but that didn't interest me for a nanosecond, although I could drive by that stage.

I'm still not sure how I passed my test the first time but I did.

Life often tends to revolve around three little words, doesn't it? I've become very used to them being 'f**k off Fletch' but when you're talking about learning to drive, those three little words are always 'mirror, signal, manoeuvre'. It's drilled into everyone who has ever got behind the wheel of a car.

My instructor felt that I was ready to take the exam and off we went, to a place near the Queen's Medical Centre in Nottingham.

I'd passed the theory test first time, proved I could see by reading the registration number of a parked car and got in. Clunk click.

'In your own time, Mr Fletcher.'

I flicked the indicator and pulled away. What mirror? I hadn't even given it a second's thought.

Immediately I knew I'd cocked up. I felt like stopping and pleading my case but knew it was pointless. I hadn't looked in the mirror and knew it would be a certain fail.

I resigned myself to that fact and just chilled, using the rest of the test as a practice for the inevitable next one.

I was so relaxed that over the next 40 minutes I did everything perfectly. Not a whiff of an error. Textbook stuff.

What a shame I'd cocked up at the start, I thought.

Anyhow, we got back to the test centre and matey congratulated me on how well I'd driven and told me that I'd passed.

Whether he hadn't noticed me giving the mirror a swerve at the start or whether I'd won him over by the rest of my driving I'll never know but I'd passed and that was all that mattered.

Although I couldn't wait to get my own wheels, I didn't want them to be a Nottingham City Transport Routemaster bus.

Two brothers who lived across the road gave me some food for thought. Leigh got a job in the prison service and gave me enough encouragement to think that I could also pursue a career there. I filled in and sent off all the application forms but nothing came of it.

His older brother Darren joined the police force and that also gave me something to consider but my cricket was taking off at the same time and in truth, that was all I wanted to do in the summer months.

I had to keep earning though and was advised that Hooters were on the lookout for staff.

An American restaurant chain – a diner, if you will – Hooters had opened a branch on London Road in Nottingham, quite close to Notts County's ground.

Chicken wings, burgers, fries and the likes were featured on the menu but the other attractions were the television sets showing wall-to-wall sport from around the globe – and the girls.

Hooters' girls were all dressed similarly, in a company-branded vest and very tight and very short shorts.

My uniform was slightly different. They gave me a shirt that had the company motto on it, 'Delightfully tacky, yet unrefined'.

I was already a big lad and someone cruelly pointed out on the first day that I had bigger boobs than any of the girls.

At first they put me in the back, out of sight, doing menial but important tasks like prepping the salad. You'd be surprised how much salad they get through each day. An entire shift of chopping onions, tomatoes and lettuce would simply fly by.

Then I progressed to the fryers, firstly doing chicken wings and then on to the prize position of flipping burgers.

This was done in full sight of the paying customers and was guaranteed to include a lot of good-natured banter, especially when anyone came in who knew me.

* * *

Mark James: Hooters' general manager in Nottingham: 'He came down to see me about the job and was clearly a big unit. I knew that he wanted to be a cricketer really, so wondered how much he wanted the job or did he just want to come and have some banter with the girls?

'I took him through into the back and introduced him to our kitchen manager, Alex Holmes.

'Alex was from Birmingham and ran a tight ship, he was brutal with any slackers. He'd been a head chef at a high end restaurant and wasn't going to let his standards slip for a kid from Bulwell.

'He looked at me and I could tell what he was thinking. I said, "Don't worry, he'll get stuck in."

'The last thing I saw was Alex giving Fletch a bag of Spanish onions and a box of tomatoes. He explained exactly how he wanted them chopping.

'When he returned to the scene it was carnage, as Fletch had ignored the advice and done his own thing.

'My kitchen manager tore a proper strip off him, really came down hard on him. Fletch's response? "I don't see the problem," he said. "They're only onions and tomatoes!"

'They got along fine after that, especially once Alex had let it be known that he was a huge cricket fan. Fletch graduated on to the fryers and became very popular with everyone that came in. He was a great team player, very polite and totally reliable.

'I've enjoyed following his success ever since and it's always good fun whenever he comes back to see us. He's never far from our thoughts because my wife and I named our Cavachon pup "Fletcher".'

* * *

It was good fun at Hooters and filled the void until I was offered something more permanent by Notts. In fact, shortly after signing my first cricket contract I was asked to go back there and do a little interview with Sky Sports, which they turned into a really nice piece, with me pretending to cook chicken wings.

I'd got into Notts' seconds by this stage and at the end of the season they said they wanted to keep an eye on me and wanted me to work on my fitness with the first team.

Naturally, I was very happy that my cricket was moving in the right direction but I was concerned that there was no promise of any money coming my way at this stage.

I still needed to hand over something for my board and needed to catch buses to and from the ground.

My concerns were passed to Wayne Noon (Noony), who was looking after the second team at this stage and he agreed to talk to Mick Newell, the club's director of cricket.

A solution was found but it meant some early morning starts for me. The new stand on the Bridgford Road side of the ground was being built and the workmen needed early access, so from around 7am until 1pm I worked on the gates, continually opening and closing them as the lorries delivered their loads and went out again.

I did that for the full winter but hated it because it was so cold. They'd provided me with a little shed to sit in and occasionally I would be relieved from my post but only to go and help with some essential maintenance work around the ground, stuff like changing light bulbs or painting.

Once my shift had finished on the gates I would then go and join the first team squad, either in the nets or the gym and work through the afternoon with them.

Noony was a very important person in my life at that stage and did so much to accelerate my progress towards becoming a first-class cricketer.

* * *

Wayne Noon: 'Phil de Freitas recommended Fletch to us and I went and saw him playing for Papplewick and Linby. He didn't get any wickets that day but he did okay and I thought he was worth keeping an eye on.

'I asked him to come down to Trent Bridge, it was towards the end of the season and we were weighing all of the players.

'We got him on the scales and he was 125kg. I recall him saying, "Is that good?"

'"There's no other bowler at Trent Bridge over 100kg, so I guess you're winning!" I replied.

'I ran some fitness sessions for the players around that time and set out a few circuits in the Woodhead Hall. Fletch was invited to come down and join in.

'Beside each activity was a laminate explaining what needed to be done. I blew the whistle to start and immediately heard Fletch yell, "Noony, can you come and hold my feet, I can't get up."

'He was only supposed to be doing sit-ups!'

* * *

I worked hard on my fitness that winter and remained determined to make the most of the chance that Noony and the rest of the coaching staff had given me.

I'd like to think I was showing them something in the nets and was given a lovely surprise when they asked me to go on the pre-season tour to South Africa, as I'd only ever been to Spain before that.

It possibly came about because Charlie Shreck had been called into the England Lions squad that were touring India.

We were based at the High Performance Centre in Pretoria and I discovered that each day tended to follow a similar weather pattern. There would be heavy rainfall for a while, then it would get sweltering hot and it would stay like that, right through the night.

Someone in charge, in their infinite wisdom, had decided that it would be a good idea to put myself and Mark Wagh (Waggy) in the same room.

Waggy had served the county with great distinction for several years after doing the same with Warwickshire but we were polar opposites in most respects. That was certainly true when it came to feeling the heat.

It was sweltering for much of our time in South Africa, permanently around 30-odd degrees. I was roasting hot and couldn't sleep at night because of it. Even so, he wouldn't let me have the air conditioning on.

Waggy reckoned it dried your throat out and made you ill, so he wouldn't hear of it. As a youngster on his first trip, my opinion counted for nothing.

I really liked him but that was a long ten days without any air-con, I can tell you. Horrendous.

Despite the daily downpours we managed to get some cricket in and I acquitted myself quite well, managing to pick up a five-fer in one of the one-day practice matches, although it was played on something of a fruity pitch.

I enjoyed the trip immensely but on the final day we were all told that we would be getting an appraisal. Suddenly, it felt like school all over again.

I sat nervously around the swimming pool with a couple of the other lads, Ian Saxelby and Andy Carter, wondering what would happen.

Sax was called away first and after 20 minutes or so he came back, absolutely buzzing. He'd been given a six-month contract.

Then Carts went, he came back with a three-month deal. My heart sank because I felt that as they had left me until last it meant I wasn't going to get picked. 'No chance,' I thought, as I went off to find out my fate.

Mick Newell, Wayne Noon and the rest of the coaching staff were there and it couldn't have gone any better because they gave me a deal for the forthcoming season, on something like five or six grand.

I certainly owe Mick for taking that early punt on me.

* * *

Mick Newell: 'We took some extra bowlers on that trip to South Africa and they were all very different from each other.

'Carts had a bit of pace, Sax was more of an all-rounder and Fletch was the sort of bowler that we thought would be a steady, stick it around the top of off stump sort of guy who would go well at Trent Bridge and in English conditions and consistently not go for more than around two and a half runs an over.

'That's exactly how it panned out and over ten years his career record has been outstanding.'

* * *

I couldn't believe they'd given me that contract at first and I was especially delighted because another lad I got along with, by the name of Alex Hales, had also been handed a deal.

He'd impressed the coaching staff throughout the previous season and now we were all going to start life together as professional cricketers.

I was even offered a choice of available squad numbers and asked to choose one. As I was 19 at the time I thought I'd take that and it's remained with me throughout my career.

3

Into The System

I'D FIRST become involved with cricket when a mate of mine, Dick Bramley, asked if I fancied helping out at my local club, Bulwell CC, as they were short-handed.

I was only 12 or so but thoroughly enjoyed it and stayed for a couple of seasons before being attracted to one of the larger clubs in the area.

Papplewick and Linby CC were around five miles away but had a good record of developing youngsters and had several age group sides, all playing competitive cricket.

I'd joined as an eager under-13 but by the age of 15 I was in the first team, playing in the Notts Premier League, the highest level of club cricket in the county.

Eager as I was to have a bowl each week, I'd often have to wait a while for my turn because our opening bowlers were former England Test star Phil de Freitas and left-arm quick Mark Footitt, who went on to play for Notts, Derbyshire and Surrey.

As much as I loved the cricket and the social side of the sport, I always looked forward to the teas. Over the years I've often been asked about the best I've had and I'll never forget the day we went up to north-east Derbyshire to play against Killamarsh.

They managed to top everything I've ever had before or since. I'm not sure it's the most health-conscious approach to sport but it was good.

They sent someone out to the local chippy for ten big bags of chips and a load of curry sauce. Now that's quality!

Johnny Thrower was the groundsman at Papplewick and Linby and as time went by he took me under his wing and taught me some of the tricks of his trade.

He showed me how to cut the outfield and roll wickets, almost giving me an apprenticeship in his craft, although he has different memories of my early days with the club.

* * *

Johnny Thrower: 'The first time I met Luke was when I was asked to go and pick him up from Bulwell, a young lad who was just making up the numbers for the third team.

'I completely forgot all about it and by the time I'd been reminded, it was almost two hours after I should have got him.

'He was still there, sat on the railings outside the Ken Martin Leisure Centre. I couldn't believe it when I first saw him, he was a proper fat lad and was almost round to look at.

'Physically, he struggled to move but he liked his cricket and got better and better over a period of about 18 months.

'At the age of 13 he looked 17 but it was quite comical because his voice hadn't yet broken. We knew he could hit a ball and we knew he could bowl and he just kept improving beyond belief.

'He graduated quickly from the thirds, via a brief spell in the second team, into the first XI. Then he made his mark with the bat, becoming the youngest player to score a century in the Notts Premier League.

'I would always be working on the ground somewhere and for a while he would come down virtually every day to see me. He wasn't manually gifted but was always happy to help out, although his boredom span was probably only about 20 seconds at best, and some days that would be 15 seconds too long for him.'

* * *

I enjoyed the challenges that were presented each week and knew I was improving rapidly. Even so, I was still a little bit surprised when I was recommended for a trial and then got selected to play for the county under-15s.

Paul Johnson, a former Nottinghamshire captain and scorer of over 20,000 first-class runs, had recently moved into coaching and was looking after my age group.

* * *

Paul Johnson: 'I brought him into the county system at 15 and it was immediately noticeable that he was twice the size of everyone else. I called him "The Doorman".

'His club had recommended him for a trial and he was certainly a big lad but he had all the makings of a really good bowling action.

'Because of his size I thought he might even be worth two wickets every time. At that age youngsters can be intimidated by playing against someone so big.

'I often had him batting at number 12, I know he hated me for that but hopefully it inspired him to do better from then on.

'He was a lovely lad and I thought he would run through a wall backwards if he was given an opportunity.'

* * *

If anyone had any film footage of me bowling back then and compared it to my current action then you wouldn't see too much of a difference.

I mention that because everything about my action came quite naturally to me and no one has really tried to tamper with it over the years. Things always seemed to be all right as they were; perhaps that's why I haven't suffered many injuries over the years.

There were plenty of things to learn as I went along, of course. Andre Adams taught me a lot about using the crease, when to go wider and when to go tighter, that sort of thing.

I've just got more of an understanding about the art of bowling as the years have gone on.

Being honest, I would be the first to admit that my run-up isn't the most graceful thing you'll ever see on a cricket field.

I could use the excuse that invariably I'm having to run uphill and into the wind but that doesn't really excuse it.

To put my approach to the crease into words I have to defer to Paul Johnson, who gave me plenty of useful advice in those early years.

He once used the following phrase and it's generally been accepted as the best way of describing me, 'Fletch runs like he's towing a caravan.'

In my first appearance for the under-15s I justified my call-up, taking 4-35 against Derbyshire, with Ross Whiteley as my first wicket. Akhil Patel, brother of Samit, scored 85 for us in a convincing victory.

Further matches followed at that level and then I graduated into the under-17 set-up but under different coaches I didn't make the grade they were looking for and failed to win a place in the club's academy.

I'd scored my first hundred in the Notts Premier League at 17, an unbeaten 105 against Thoresby Colliery. That day I shared in a stand of 124 with Phil de Freitas and thanks to him tipping off Wayne Noon I was soon back on the county's radar.

In 2006 I made my debut for the county second XI and, fittingly, it was at my home club ground at Papplewick.

Middlesex provided the opposition and a look back at the scorecard reveals plenty of names that have become familiar over the years.

The visitors included solid county pros like Paul Weekes, Billy Godleman, Ben Scott, Chris Wright and Melvyn Betts, plus a couple of future Test players in Dawid Malan and 17-year-old Steven Finn.

Samit Patel scored 97 for us in a comfortable victory and we also had players like Gareth Clough, Russell Warren, Will Smith and Paul McMahon, who had all played for Notts, plus a South African trialist by the name of Faf du Plessis.[1]

I wonder what happened to him?

My three overs went for 21 runs and I wasn't required to bat but I'd dipped my toe in the water at this level and wanted more of it.

There was much to learn, as Wayne Noon recalls: 'We were playing in a second team match at Northampton and I went down for breakfast ahead of the final day. I was joined at the table by Fletch, Alex Hales and John Simpson, who was on trial with us before going on to have a terrific career with Middlesex.

'Fletch couldn't wait to start talking. "Noony, you missed a great night last night, we went to a club and it was mint."

'Before he could say any more, he yelped loudly. Hales had obviously whacked him under the table.

---

1 du Plessis went on to become South Africa's captain in Test, ODI and T20 cricket

Fletch still didn't get it and blurted out, "What did you do that for?"

'He didn't bowl particularly well that morning but was much better after lunch when we got the last few wickets to win the match. I thought it best to take him to one side then and explain a few things about how he should start conducting himself and how he might not want to get a reputation for dropping his mates in trouble.'

* * *

At the start of the 2008 summer I made my first-class debut for Nottinghamshire, in a rain-shortened match against Oxford University at The Parks.

It was just before the start of the County Championship season, so we had a fairly strong side out and Stuart Broad, signed during the winter from Leicestershire, was making his county debut.

It was obviously the first time that I'd played alongside Broady, who had just come to the club having made his international debut.

* * *

Stuart Broad: 'I signed for Notts at the same time as Fletch but didn't really get to know him too much during that first winter, as I was away making my debut for England in Sri Lanka and New Zealand. We both made our county debuts in that match at Oxford and I started to find out about his background and learnt all about his Hooters stuff. They told me he'd been working on the Trent Bridge gates because I'd just assumed he'd come through the academy.

'I could tell immediately that he's a warm character, an energy-giver on the field and his biggest strength is he doesn't over-think things. You get the sense he plays cricket for the love of it and feels privileged to be out there.'

* * *

Broady and Franks sent down a few overs to the university openers before I came on for my first bowl for Notts. I wasn't alone, as I was accompanied by Lady Luck.

My maiden victim was a chap called Eddie Abel, a left-handed batsman, and I don't think I've taken a wicket like it since. It was going down the leg side, struck his thigh pad and went behind his legs on to the stumps.

You take them how you can get them and it was nice to get up and running.

The rest of that season was spent learning my craft in the second string and with the England under-19s.

New Zealand toured that summer and I thoroughly enjoyed representing my country, especially as I shared the experience with county teammates Hales and Saxelby.

Among the others to feature were Chris Woakes, James Taylor, Liam Dawson and Tom Westley, who was the captain.

Our opponents also had some players who went to the very top of the game, including Kane Williamson, Jimmy Neesham and Doug Bracewell. We won the two-match Test series 1-0, courtesy of a victory at Taunton and shared the one-day series 1-1, with two matches being rained off and the other being a dramatic tie.

That match, at Hove, was perhaps my best moment. New Zealand only needed a couple of runs to win in the final over but I managed to grab a couple of wickets running up the hill, yorking Nick Beard with the penultimate ball to ensure a share of the spoils.

4

Troublemakers

THEY WERE certainly great times around then, with each week following a similar pattern. During the cricket season I'd play in a second XI championship game on Monday, Tuesday and Wednesday, then we'd generally have a one-dayer on the Thursday.

Then it was time for fuuuuuuuuuun, baby!

On Thursday nights you'd find me in the Oceana nightclub, on Friday it was the Loveshack at Nottingham's famous music venue, Rock City and Saturday would mean a trip to Walkabout, often catching up with the other lads who had been playing in the Premier League that afternoon.

I'd be involved in all sorts of crazy stunts because when you are young and foolish and out with your mates it's easy to get drawn into challenges and dares. To keep face among your peers you have to be seen to comply.

At the time there was a fairly naff dance tune by Basshunter that I liked, called 'Now You're Gone'.

Whenever we were out, every time it came on, I had to tip the drink I was holding over my head.

It took quite some time before I realised that whenever I had got a fresh pint there would be a request to play it.

You can only go on like that for so long but one of those madcap weekends was to have a profound and lasting effect upon my life.

Slightly the worse for wear, I met a young lady standing beside the red post box outside Walkabout (now the Bierkeller), on Friary Lane. We hit it off immediately and exchanged details – she told me her name was Kirsty, I told her mine was Bernard.

She still asks me why I did that but you lads will totally understand about the unwritten rule of maintaining anonymity on a first meeting, right?

Things progressed nicely from then on but it was all so long ago that I recall we used to keep in touch on MSN Messenger. Remember that?

Kirsty had no idea about cricket and certainly had no idea who I was but we've been together for more than a decade now and have two lovely children, Freddie and Rosie.

Before that happened I'd moved out of the family home in Bulwell and left behind the bunk bed I shared with my younger brother.

Sam was up there on the top bunk and I was underneath him, nicely snuggled under my Stone Cold Steve Austin duvet.

I'd been a big fan of WWE in my younger years and Stone Cold was my favourite wrestler. I'd got the full set, duvet, sheets and pillow cases. What must I have looked like?

Just before leaving home the Stone Cold set ended up in the bin after a heavy night out turned a little messy.

Given my build, I reckon I could have given wrestling a good go but life was steering me in another direction and under the same roof as Alexander Daniel Hales!

I should point out that there will inevitably be confusion from this point on because Hales is known as 'Baz' in the game.

Some of you may be familiar with the former footballer Barry Hayles, who played for such clubs as Bristol Rovers, Fulham and Millwall, plus a few others, during a lengthy and successful career.

Paul Franks is credited with starting it. Alex became Barry – and then it was shortened to Baz and stuck.

Whereas my own cricketing career was beginning to take off at my local county club, Hales was having to move lock, stock and two smoking barrels up the country from his southern roots.

He comes from Chalfont in Buckinghamshire and had already made several appearances for their side in the Minor Counties championship, as well as delivering some stunning performances while on the books of MCC Young Cricketers at Lord's.

Having seen him supply some sparkling knocks for them, while on trial, Notts had backed their judgement by snapping Hales up before any other county could.

We'd hit it off from the start and were pretty inseparable by then and took the plunge to move in together. He'd found a flat on Musters Road and was looking for someone to share with, so I asked if I could move in and the club sorted it, taking the rent out of my wages.

There were just the two of us and it was brilliant. As individuals we were both as untidy as each other, so it was organised chaos.

Despite my 'catering' background at Hooters I couldn't really cook and neither could he but we had a go whenever we had to, although more often than not we ate out. Antonio's on Trent Bridge was a favourite, or we'd try and sniff out a good deal if we could because we weren't on a great deal of money.

There was many an evening where we'd be looking across the table from each other at a Harvester's two for one deal, or if we fancied a plateful we'd be found in a Toby Carvery, piling the plate up nice and high.

I made my first-class and my one-day debuts for Notts just before Baz but he didn't waste any time in catching up.

A brilliant one-day innings of 150 against Worcestershire was caught by the television cameras and he didn't look back from then on. It was transparently clear that my housemate was going to be a major force in the game and I've enjoyed his successes. He's played some of the best innings I've been privileged to witness but above all else he's been a good mate.

During his time as an England Test player Baz showed how much our friendship was worth. I had allowed myself to be talked into doing an open question and answer session in Nottingham, for supporters, with money being raised for charity.

Despite having one or two calming drinks beforehand I was as nervous as hell as I recounted some of the stories you'll read in this book.

They were going down pretty well but after an hour or so the evening was given a real boost. Baz, midway through a Test match, had walked off the field at Edgbaston a couple of hours earlier and driven to Nottingham to support me. Additionally, he brought a signed England shirt which raised a fortune on the night.

Maybe he thought he owed me – because he'd helped get me into trouble a few times. Perhaps, if asked, he'd view it the other way around though!

One such instance came after a one-day match against Scotland at Trent Bridge. It was the old Pro 40 competition, played on a Sunday. I used to like that because we could go out the night before and still get a bit of a lie-in because the match didn't start until 2pm.

Anyway, me and Baz thought we'd go and have a few drinks on the Saturday night, nothing too big. 'We're only playing Scotland tomorrow and they're not exactly great, are they?' he quipped.

It turned into quite a big night and we were out until about half past three. We rocked up and batted first and he was immediately dismissed by a cousin of William Wallace.

Later on, I bowled like a t**t but we managed to scrape over the line and get the win. Job done, I thought, as I took a quick shower and relaxed in the dressing room with a bottle of beer. Getting up to go home, I was jolted by a command from Mick Newell.

'Fletch, come into my office.'

I walked up the couple of steps and went in. Hales was already sat there, so alarm bells were starting to ring. 'Oh s**t, what's going on here?' I thought.

I sat down close to Baz and the interrogation began.

'What were you two doing last night?' said Mick.

We glanced towards each other and I offered, 'We just went out for a meal and a couple of drinks.'

'Oh yeah, what time did you get in?'

We looked at each other again and I said, 'Oh, about half ten or 11 o'clock Mick, something like that.'

Our gaffer glared and offered accusingly, 'No, you didn't.'

I was starting to become worried now because I knew we had been dropped in it somehow. Again there was a look between us. Baz wasn't giving me much to work with here, so I tried again. 'Oh, sorry, maybe it was about one o'clock then, yeah it was one.'

He went, 'No you f*****g weren't, you were seen out at around half past three this morning, so let's have the truth.'

We'd been rumbled but didn't have to wait long before finding out by whom.

'A son of one of the committee saw you both out in the Loveshack.'

Then he started having at go at Halesy, really laying into him. Out of the corner of my eye I could see my housemate's bottom lip starting to twitch as he was given the mother of all rollickings. It wasn't funny – but it was, so I started to smirk at his discomfort.

Remember, I'm 20 years old and had just signed my first contract. Then I started to laugh as the volley continued, knowing full well that it would be my turn next.

That time was now.

'What the f**k are you laughing at? Look at the state of you, you are a new pro and a disgrace, disrespecting me, your teammates and the club.'

Whether it was through nerves, fear or sheer stupidity, I don't know why but I'm laughing even more at this stage.

Having taken his medicine, Baz had his head down by now, determined not to make eye contact with me.

Laughing, I could just about splurt out, 'I'm sorry, I'm sorry.'

Our discomfort was brought to a swift conclusion with only five more words.

'Get out and go home.'

Driving home, I played out the scenario again in my mind. I wasn't sure if that was it or there'd be further punishment or perhaps a fine or suspension, so decided to ring Mick and find out how much trouble I was in.

'I'm really sorry and I couldn't help laughing. I just used to get the giggles a lot at school and can't control it.'

His response was brief, 'Just don't do it again,' as he slammed the phone down.

That certainly wasn't the only time I had to apologise to Mick Newell and I can only be thankful that usually he'd be there to cover if we'd got into any scrapes.

* * *

Mick Newell: 'My general recollection of that period is that whenever I had to give Fletch a bollocking, he ended up either giggling or laughing.

'It's not the sort of response you want but you can't help but love him.

'It took him a long time to realise that he was well known in Nottingham and that if he went out in the city then people would recognise him.

'For a long time I think he still thought he was a Saturday afternoon club cricketer and it took him a long time to realise how well known he was. If he went out people would recognise him and if he caused mayhem, well, they knew who he was and they'd ring me and tell me.

'One of the problems with him and Hales was that they didn't have girlfriends at the time, they just had each other for company, so made a habit of getting each other into trouble.

'I don't think they ever did anything that was hugely dangerous, although there was one occasion when I had to fend off *The Sun* newspaper, who were enquiring about the pair of them!'

5

From Heroes To Teammates

CONSIDERING THAT only a year or so earlier I had been watching on as a fan, it was all a little surreal to go into the Notts dressing room and be stood next to the likes of Mark Ealham, Graeme Swann, Ryan 'Siddy' Sidebottom and Chris Read.

They had been among my sporting heroes but were now teammates, as I began to make my way in the game. Swanny was a bit of a clown but they were all good senior players to be around and the dressing room was as good as it has been while I've been playing.

Through necessity, a lot of my time would be spent with the other bowlers and they were some of the very best to learn from, although perhaps I didn't always appreciate it at the time.

The cumulative experience of players such as Ealham, Sidebottom, Andre Adams, Paul Franks and Ali Brown were never shy in letting me know if I'd stepped out of line or they thought I wasn't giving of my best.

They were all hard but fair and had a winning mentality. Ealy took to me and I loved watching him go about his work and tried to imitate a lot of what he did.

He was one of the very best death bowlers around and I used that as a benchmark, promising to myself that I needed to be as good as, if not better, than him.

By that stage of his career his England days were behind him but he was still one of the best operators around. I looked at the length of his career and wondered how he'd managed to keep going at that level of consistency for more than two decades.

'Easy,' he'd say. 'Whatever the fitness guys ask of you, just give them eight out of ten.'

I was never sure if he was kidding or not but I've always remembered that quote, although it's not something that does it for me.

I've always been a big lad and have always had to put the hard work in during training; you probably get more enjoyment out of it as well if you're giving 100 per cent.

It was clearly different in Ealy's day.

* * *

Mark Ealham: 'I was a massive fan of being fit enough to play cricket. They were different times and it was a different generation but I was always a massive fan of being fit enough to play cricket, fit enough to bat or bowl.

'Do what you needed to do to get ready but always save enough for the match. There were always players who would warm up like lunatics but to my way of thinking that would always take a percentage out of you.

'Warm-up is called a warm-up for a reason!

'Halfway through my career things became a little more professional with regards to training but I was still "old-school" and that meant the fitness coach was always on my back.

'If he wanted 12 from the beep test, I'd give him 12.1. There would then be a conversation about, "Is there more in the tank?"

'I'd always reply, "Yes, but I'm saving it for another time!"

'I might have been lucky but I seldom missed matches through injury because of it, my name would always be on the sheet and I would pass advice like that on to Fletch.

'Mick Newell probably didn't like it, he would have preferred his senior pros to be passing on good advice to the youngsters but Fletch knew what I was getting at.

'Always save your main energy for playing, don't leave too much of it in the gym.'

Ealy also remembers that I was never too far away from trouble during those early days in the first team: 'My first recollection of seeing him around the place was not only of thinking what a huge bloke he was but also that he made his presence felt.

'It was always him and Hales, collectively they were known as either Batman and Robin or Pinky and Perky, but they always seemed to be involved in some caper or another.

'It became a regular thing from the dressing room to be able to watch the pair of them going up the stairs to Mick's office.

'I'd usually be sat near the door with Mark Wagh, we'd have a giggle at them and probably reminisce about our own youth and similar experiences.

'They'd always be looking pretty glum when they went in, we'd then hear Mick ranting and raving at them and a few seconds later out they'd come. Their latest misdemeanour over and done with.'

* * *

Ryan Sidebottom was in and out of the team when I was first starting, often spending lengthy periods away with England. When he was around he was terrific, although could be a real grump at times.

He was quite an emotional guy but always up for a laugh as well. Get on the wrong side or try and play a prank on him and you'd be sure to find the toes cut out of your socks pretty soon afterwards.

Andre Adams is the best bowler I've worked with, no doubt, and he was also Notts through and through.

Although he must have worked incredibly hard to get to the level that he did, a lot of it came so naturally to him that he was always pretty perplexed as to why others couldn't do it as well.

He could never get his head around why others weren't able to execute their skills as easily as he did and it often led to him venting his frustrations.

A proper senior player, 'Dre' would think nothing of pulling you up if he thought you were slacking. Frequently, that would mean me being in the firing line, often in the dressing room in full view of the others.

I would think, 'Here we go, he's picking on me again.' But he wasn't, he just cared so much and it took a while for that to sink in.

What a man, as loyal a player as the county have ever had and you couldn't wish to have anyone better in your corner.

* * *

Andre Adams: 'I think the world of Fletch, everyone knows him as such a funny and loveable man but he's also a very genuine guy.

'The first time I met him was for an early season second team game, I'd just flown back and needed a match to get prepared.

'I could tell he had the makings of a very decent cricketer. He was a gifted young man, with good ability, good hands and he could bat.

'I could tell he had a nice character and would put it in for you but he was different.

'Charlie Shreck and I were old-school and he wasn't ready for that sort of approach, which I respected in a strange sort of way, although I also found it a bit confronting at times.

'He got into a few scrapes early on but you can't help but love him, even after he'd committed a misdemeanour.'

* * *

Charlie Shreck was another member of the fast bowlers' union and another that I enjoyed spending time with. The big Cornishman was a big influence on me because I could see how hard he worked.

He was of the opinion that the more you bowled, the better you'd be. Shrecky loved nothing more than bowling lengthy spells and when he got it right he was as good as any around.

On his day he was top-class, bowling with decent pace and with the ability to move the ball both ways.

Like many of the others he could be grumpy at times but he was a big influence in showing me how to recover properly after bowling a lot of overs.

He was a strong believer in using pool sessions to aid recovery and loved to be first in the pool early the next morning.

Paul Franks has become something of a Nottinghamshire legend. Like me, born and bred in the county and fiercely proud of his heritage.

He could be pretty fiery, another one that could go berserk on the field when the mood took him. He'd played for England earlier in his career but by the time I joined him in the team he was just about the best number eight batsman in the country, very reliable.

Franksy – also known as 'The General' – made such a good job of it, that for a while our coaching staff thought he was being wasted down there and he was promoted to opener.

We had a big spat once. As usual, it was my fault and the passing years have made me understand a little more.

It was against Surrey at Trent Bridge and Titch (James Taylor) had taken over as captain at the last minute, with Chris Read pulling out through injury.

Titch brought me on for one over, then took me off again.

I wasn't happy about the decision and was ticking; really close to losing it. The theory, I was told, was that he wanted to squeeze in one more over before a break. It didn't make any sense to me so I wouldn't let it drop, I was spewing at being taken off.

It was nothing to do with Franksy but he intervened, telling me to shut it and get on with the game. He was a senior player and was quite within his rights to take me to task over the way I was acting.

I realise that now and 100 per cent endorse it but back then I was young and stupid and we both said a few things.

We won the game, so it was all quickly forgotten – until now, when I've just remembered it!

* * *

Paul Franks: 'You must have respect for the captaincy and Fletch probably wouldn't have done it had Readie been in charge.

'Titch had made the decision and I know from my own personal experience that kicking off with the captain is not a track to go down. It's something I've fallen foul of in the past and you learn from it and move to a position where you can give people the benefit of your own experience.

'Fletch is now in that position, a senior member of the side, who would manage that same situation differently now.

'That aside, I've always been proud of him. I was very happy to see another home-grown boy come through like he did.

'He made inroads quickly, impressing in club cricket, through the seconds and into the firsts, where he soon grasped that he had it within him to become a very good cricketer.'

* * *

Ali Brown came to Trent Bridge after a long and successful career with Surrey. We hit it off straight away and would regularly start our day with an early morning session in the Trent Bridge gym together.

* * *

Ali Brown: 'When I moved to Notts it meant that I'd swapped my hour and a quarter commute to The Oval for a five-minute ride into Trent Bridge and I decided to use that spare hour for some gym time.

'I roped Fletch in to help, often bribing him with a promise of a sandwich from the No.8 deli after we'd done. It worked out well for both of us actually, I think he thought I was quite old and wanted to look after me!

'Him and Alex Hales were often in trouble and then always had to own up to what they'd done. I'd see them trooping off to

Mick's door, it was like being summoned to see the headmaster. They'd come out as white as a sheet.

'I think that's what made Mick such a good manager, he had a certain fear about him but would get it all sorted out and move on as quickly as possible.

'Certainly his style of management helped Fletch out in the early years.'

* * *

I think when Ali first met Kirsty he thought she had a vendetta against him. One day she nearly set him on fire. We were sat in a pub, the Royal Oak at Radcliffe-on-Trent, with Ali opposite us.

For some reason we'd got some pork scratchings in a brown paper bag. There was a candle on the table and the bag got too close to it and set alight.

Kirsty instinctively tried to put out the flames and proceeded to waft the burning embers all over Ali.

To compound matters, the following day Ali was wearing flip-flops when Kirsty accidentally dropped a Corona beer bottle on his toe!

There were lots of other strong characters around in my formative years at the club and I'm sure many will crop up as we continue this look back. Before we go any further, though, I must mention Rob Ferley.

A left-arm spinner, he'd moved up to Trent Bridge from Kent but had limited opportunities to impress in the first team, with Samit, Swanny, or both, ahead of him in the pecking order.

Rob and I played a fair amount of second-team cricket together and got on pretty well. One winter, the one where I was working on the gates, he got himself fixed up with some club cricket in Perth, Australia.

Likely to be away for several months, he kindly lent me his beloved car for that period. It was a red Renault Clio, which he lovingly called Reggie, and even paid the insurance for me.

Like a lot of us, Rob had a strong dislike for people who couldn't park properly.

'Why can't they park within the lines?' he'd scream most days on entering the changing rooms.

It got so bad that he started to look for bad parkers whenever he went to supermarkets. Anyone that had ventured across into two spaces would have a surprise when they returned to their vehicle.

He would unlock Reggie's boot and squeeze so tightly into the gap that was left, then climb over the back seats and out of the car through the boot.

The other person would, effectively, be pinned in and left very frustrated – and hopefully much wiser!

Rob was prone to the odd act of eccentricity. One evening he came round at about 9pm and asked me to come down to the local gym with him.

For reasons I've never fully discovered we then spent an hour wrestling each other in the baby pool.

6

You Thick T**t

I WAS playing in only my fifth first-class match when I very nearly achieved something remarkable. I scored 92.

My only previous visits to the middle in County Championship cricket had delivered scores of 8* and 0*, so I'm certain casual observers wouldn't have been expecting too much when I made my way out to join Mark Ealham on the opening day of a match against Hampshire at the Rose Bowl (as it was then called) in Southampton.

The board read 147/7 and we were up against it.

Before I'd even faced a delivery I got myself into a spot of bother with the opposition. New to the first-class game, I hadn't been made aware that on occasions the pitch inspectors would come out with the ground staff before a match and take a small sample of the playing strip away for analysis.

This is done by inserting a small plunger into the ground and withdrawing it with the sample secured. They usually will do this twice, one near each end of the strip.

Naturally, this is done away from the area where we'd run or where the ball might pitch. I'd never seen it before, as I say, but after taking guard from the umpire I noticed a small hole about a third of the way down, just at the side of the cut strip. It looked odd to me and I bellowed out my thoughts.

'Hey Ealy, there's a hole here,' I laughed towards my teammate, loud enough for everyone to hear.

'Yes, and there's one at this end you thick t**t,' bellowed Dominic Cork, Hampshire's former England all-rounder who is well known for his fiery attitude out on the pitch.

Corky had spent most of his career playing for Derbyshire and loved nothing more than a good scrap against their traditional rivals.

Quite what he made of me getting so many runs isn't clear but he was in no mood for any fun when I reached 80. Armed with a second new ball he popped in three slips and a gully but proceeded to give me a barrage of bumpers. Every ball was banged in short at me.

'Why don't you pitch it up and bowl to your field?' I cheekily offered.

He went ballistic.

'Who the f**k do you think you are, coming out here giving it...'

I was out of order really, just new to the game and being disrespectful to someone who had achieved so much in the sport. Corky is an absolute legend and I've enjoyed catching up with him ever since – but on that day he'd have killed me if he could.

I'd started my innings nicely and felt pretty good early on, timing one or two sweetly which always helps.

Ealy kept chatting as we went along, getting me through to a maiden fifty, into the 60s, then 70s, 80s and on to 92.

At that point I was certainly thinking of the repercussions if I could register a maiden hundred. 'They'll be calling me the next Flintoff,' I thought to myself.

Someone on the field even said that I was batting like Wally Hammond but that went over my head – I had no idea then who that gentleman was.

Self-consciously I just presumed the inference was that he was a big chap but he turns out he was just a very good batsman, scoring over 7,000 runs for England.

It was another international cricketer who ended my fun. I'd managed to connect with a few and hit Imran Tahir away for three big sixes before he pushed one through a little bit quicker – I think it was his slider – and the South African leg-spinner broke my defences and my heart by bowling me.

Although I was disappointed to get out when in sight of such an important milestone, I was also quite proud of what I'd achieved so early in my career, especially as we went on to win the match.

Afterwards, some people were getting a little giddy by referring to me as the next big thing in terms of being an all-rounder but it took me another ten years before I reached 92 again and I'm still waiting for that elusive first three-figure score.

Nevertheless, I was pleased to have scored a few runs for the side and privileged to have spent time batting alongside Ealy.

* * *

Mark Ealham: 'I'd just gone in at number eight and normally when I was left with the tail I'd start to have a swish and a swing but I had confidence in him.

'"What are we doing, Ealy?" he said in his broad Nottingham accent.

'I can remember the "holes" conversation clearly and it gave Corky the opportunity to have a pop at him but I told Fletch to ignore him, be comfortable and play his own game.

'He played really well from then on and soon took over the partnership. We had one discussion about facing Imran Tahir. I was concerned if he just prodded and poked around then he might be in trouble, so urged him to be positive.

'Fletch responded by slog-sweeping the spinner for six and followed it up by hitting a full toss for four.

'I thought he'd certainly get to his hundred and remember feeling gutted when he got out.

'I've watched his career with interest since then and despite his soft exterior, he is a tough lad at heart and has become a really good bowler.'

7

What A Bonus

AFTER FINISHING as runners-up to Durham in 2008 and 2009, Nottinghamshire went one better and lifted the County Championship title in 2010.

I started that season in the team but came in and out through the course of the campaign, playing a part here and there and watching from the sidelines on other occasions.

We'd been front-runners throughout but a heavy home defeat by Yorkshire in the penultimate match set us back. With Ryan Sidebottom returning to the team from England duty, to play his final match for the county, I lost my place for the all-important trip to Old Trafford to face Lancashire.

It was now a three-horse race for the title. We were still top of the table but had Somerset and Yorkshire breathing down our necks, with only seven points separating the sides.

Those four September days in Manchester are now etched in the county's folklore, but for the most part, they were hugely frustrating.

It rained and rained and rained and a lot of cards were dealt inside our dressing room. Only one over was possible on the first day and not much more on the second. Ironically, as the match neared the halfway point, the sun came out for the first time but was so low in the sky it was in the eyes of the batsmen and forced the players from the field.

This is totally true and is the reason that after 150 years of playing with the square running from east to west they decided to rotate it by 90 degrees that winter.

The third day was washed out as well, so there were lots of discussions about what we should do during our team meal on the third evening.

All turned out well in the end, with us getting the necessary bonus points and draw that we needed after the other matches had also gone our way.

Adam Voges and Samit Patel – helped by a nervy last-wicket partnership between Sidebottom and Darren Pattinson – got us to the 400 we needed and then we took three Lancashire wickets quickly to lift the title.

Fearful of time running out on us, Mick Newell had despatched all the non-playing members of the dressing room all around Old Trafford to act as ball boys if needed, in order to keep the game moving quickly.

Those of us not directly involved, Andy Carter, Scott Elstone, Graeme White and myself, were spaced all around the ground and when Andre Adams took the decisive wicket he ran in my direction which helps explain why I was one of the first on the scene to begin the celebrations.

'It was just a reaction, pure relief from me at getting the wicket and realising what it meant. I ran down towards fine leg and suddenly there was Fletch, grabbing me tightly and he wouldn't let go. He was as happy as anyone and that's how it should be,' Dre now recalls.

That same day, 16 September 2010, was also the day that Andrew 'Freddie' Flintoff retired from all cricket. He hadn't played much that season and had made the announcement during the final session of the match.

I remember how generous he was towards us that day and enjoyed spending a little bit of time with him and sharing a huge cigar on the balcony afterwards.

With hindsight I probably didn't respect our championship win enough at the time, as I thought this was the norm. We got a £12,000 bonus each for winning it and when you are only on a few thousand for the season that was incredible.

Some of the players and people we had in that team were just phenomenal, so it was great to share a championship win with them. I wish I'd respected it a little bit more at the time because some guys go a whole career without winning a trophy.

As the years have passed I've realised more and more how difficult it is to win the title and would love to think I could do it again before my days are over but to do it in my first full year was amazing.

With a few quid in my pocket it was time for some new gear as I wanted to look the part, although the club's press officer Michael Temple remembers it very differently: 'I warmed to Fletch straightaway as a lad who hadn't come into cricket via the normal route. He didn't seem to know how to react around some of the others but it's not surprising, there were some big characters in that Notts dressing room.

'After the championship win in 2010 he had a bit of cash to splash and disappeared down to the Victoria Centre in Nottingham to spend some of it.

'He had the entire commercial office in stitches when he returned with Andy Carter and the pair of them were dressed head to toe in G-Star gear.

'It was a popular brand at the time and every 15-year old in the land would aspire to wear a G-Star hoodie. Fletch and Carts had blown about £300 each to be about five years behind the times!'

Temps was also the person responsible for creating a nickname that has stuck with me throughout my career.

I'll let him explain, 'We started doing matchday programmes for some of the white-ball matches and popped a full colour poster of a player in the centre pages of each.

'It was just something for the youngsters to get autographs on and keep.

'To make them a little more appealing we gave each player a nickname. It was all fairly innocuous stuff, based on where they had come from.

'Jake Ball became the "Welbeck Wizard" and Andy Carter was the "Bardney Bullet" but the one for Luke was an instant hit.

'Everyone at the club still knows him as the "Bulwell Bomber".'

8

Making My Mark Down Under

WITHIN A few days of winning the title in 2010 I was off on a big adventure. I was heading to Australia, on my own, to play for Buckley Ridges, a club side based in the suburbs of Melbourne.

Nottinghamshire had developed a strong relationship with the Bucks and I was following in the footsteps of Paul Franks as their overseas pro for the forthcoming Australian winter.

I'd been to Oz a couple of times before, briefly in each of the previous two winters, heading to the Darren Lehmann Cricket Academy in Adelaide.

That had been a very different experience, as everything was regimented and organised for me. I had a schedule, which had to be strictly adhered to.

Joe Root, Alex Hales, Monty Panesar, Adam Lyth and Jake Ball are some of the English players to have been there and each of them will happily say how much it has benefitted their career.

When I went to the academy the bowling coach was Jason Gillespie and the batting coach was Greg Blewett, two players steeped in the finest traditions of Australian cricket.

I remember flying over there the first time and fretting all the way out because I had to change planes at Singapore. How do you transfer planes? Where do I go? I was genuinely shi**ing myself but it all worked out fine in the end.

I had been told that I'd be at the academy, learning new skills, from Monday to Friday each week, and then heading off to play for a local club side at weekends.

They had assigned me to a club called Sturt District CC. I didn't know what to expect but got a friendly greeting as I arrived there.

'Hi mate, I'm Shaun,' said a big, strong-looking lad, whose face seemed vaguely familiar.

It took a while for the penny to drop (it usually does with me) but when someone shouted, 'Well bowled Taity,' as he fired down an early Exocet, I realised that my warm welcome had come from Australian Test bowler Shaun Tait.

Shaun had made his Test debut at Trent Bridge during the 2005 Ashes, so we had something in common as we chatted later. Nottingham turned out to be good for him a few years later, as he took a hat-trick at Trent Bridge playing against us for Essex.

During my time in Adelaide Alex Hales had kindly driven across from Melbourne to see me (and slept on my room floor) and he was there again to greet me when I arrived for my first stint with Buckley Ridges.

Hales was also playing club cricket in Melbourne and had sorted out my accommodation, sharing with him and Wayne White (the former Derbyshire, Leicestershire and Lancashire player).

It was chaos. I was used to sharing with Hales but Wayne was something else!

I'd been expecting the same sort of regimented lifestyle that I'd experienced in Adelaide. This was completely different.

For a start it took me ages to get over the jet-lag because we just kept going out to the casino every night until all hours.

We had the cricket at weekends but in truth we weren't taking anything as seriously as we should have been during the rest of the week.

This carried on until Christmas, when Johnny Thrower, my mate from Papplewick and Linby, came over. Things hotted up even more then.

Just over the road was Johnny's Grog Shop and it had the right name because every day Johnny would go and get a slab of Pure Blonde beer and we'd sit and drink it together.

Things had to change and I needed to start applying myself properly and made the decision to move out.

Chris Rattle pretty much ran the Buckley Ridges club and he had a big property at the Patterson River Golf Club. He invited me to move in with him and from then on I started to dedicate myself to getting fit.

A visit to the scales told me how much work would be needed. I've heard all the gags before:

'What happens when Luke Fletcher steps on the scales?'

'It says "One At A Time Please"!'

'What happens when Luke Fletcher steps on the scales?'

'It says "Warning Heavy Load".'

There were no laughs to be had as I stared at the truth – I needed to shed around 14kg.

It was time for some discipline in my life.

There was a massive lake at the golf club, around 6km in length. I challenged myself to run round it every day, losing weight and building up my fitness nicely.

Chris always spurred me on but also found fun in my fitness regime.

* * *

Chris Rattle: 'Fletch arrived at Buckley with clear instructions from Notts that he had to return to Trent Bridge weighing no more than a svelte 105kg.

'After his Christmas excesses he really knuckled down – firstly by going on a diet of one can of beans plus fruit a day, but also by running, swimming and playing golf.

'The beach was at Bonbeach, just a stone's throw away from where he lived, so he'd regularly go there. *Bondi Rescue* was a popular TV programme at the time and Fletch reckoned he could do that job, so started calling himself "Bonbeach Rescue".'

* * *

That New Year's Eve I was on the beach and was fortunate to escape a nasty injury. One group were messing about with fireworks nearby and one went off and flew straight towards me, hitting me in the chest.

I was pretty lucky to avoid some serious damage but it knocked me off my feet and cut me quite badly.

* * *

There was another English lad playing at Buckley, called Rollo Sharma. Chris recalls that he set me a challenge one day, 'My brother Tim had an exercise bike upstairs at his house but there was no air-conditioning in there and one day it must have been about 45 degrees.

'Rollo challenged Fletch to ride the bike for an hour, while dressed in plastic garbage bags. So big, bold Fletch wrapped himself in garbage bags and got on the bike.

'He pedalled steadily for an hour, by which time a pool of water had collected under him on the floor, and when he ripped off the plastic bags, his body was awash in sweat.

'He not only won himself 50 dollars for the challenge but also shed about 5kg in the process. Fletch saw it as being win, win!'

* * *

Good things started to happen from then on. We had a good run in the local T20 competition and got through to the final, which was played at the Melbourne Cricket Ground.

This was an insanely good experience and one of many memorable visits to the mighty MCG.

I had managed to get tickets to go to the Boxing Day Test and it was unreal to be there in a crowd of 100,000 people as England won the Ashes.

I was also there when Australia played against Pakistan on the day that Shaun Tait bowled the fastest official ball in Test match history.

David Hussey, a Nottinghamshire teammate, kindly helped out with tickets whenever I was struggling, although I'd been reluctant to ask him at first.

Huss, or Russ as I called him (don't ask), is a proper cricketing superstar, one of the best I've played alongside and also one of the best blokes I've met.

Over the course of a decade he remained incredibly loyal to Nottinghamshire, returning whenever his international commitments would allow. No wonder I was in awe of him at first.

So, not surprisingly, it wouldn't enter my head to pester him for tickets or anything like that. I assumed his world wasn't my world. I quickly learned that Russ didn't see it that way.

* * *

David Hussey: 'What can you say about Luke Fletcher?

'Luke is the player in the dressing room that all players gravitate towards as he is hilarious, unpredictable and a big softy at heart. Luke has an infectious personality and is often the life and heartbeat of the dressing room.

'When he first joined Notts, I didn't really know him that well, so little in fact that I didn't even know that he had travelled to Australia to play club cricket over the winter.

'So, when I arrived back at Trent Bridge for the following season and found out, I felt awful.

'I asked him why he hadn't let me know and he just said, "I didn't want to bother you."

'Throughout 2010 I stumbled on the fact that he was coming over again, to play for Buckley Ridges, about 20 minutes away from me. Hales was also coming, so I asked them to stay in touch.

'They messaged me and came over for dinner and then I sorted them out with tickets for an international T20 against Pakistan, that I was fortunate enough to play in.

'That night was extremely chilly, only around 15 degrees or so and at the MCG 15 degrees only ever feels like ten degrees.

'The MCG training nets are below the street, which means that they're visible to the spectators from above, people can look down and have a bird's eye view of the players netting and preparing to play.

'The crowd was building and there would have been a few hundred people watching us warm up but through the normal chatter I heard this thick Nottingham accent, "All right Russ (for some reason Luke always called me Russ)?"

'I looked up to see Luke and Alex watching the Aussies and Pakistani players hit up. They were wearing jeans and a polo shirt, the bare minimum to pass the MCG dress code standard.

'Delighted to see them, I asked if they'd brought jumpers along, as I could see it was going to be a chilly one.

'Luke quickly responded with, "What are you talking about, Russ, this is a balmy night in Nottingham!"

'Fletch is definitely a "bloke's bloke" and the life of the dressing room but he's become a very fine first-class professional.

'It's been a privilege watching him develop from the carefree lad that he once was to the loving partner and father that he is today. Fletch is one of the best people I have met in cricket.'

9

Doing It For The Bucks

IT WAS great to be able to get out and witness some amazing live sport in Australia, going with Chris Rattle to see the Melbourne Cup horse race and to the Aussie Rules football final.

Kirsty came out to see me for a few weeks and we managed to have a little break, going to sample the delights of Sydney and Brisbane for the first time.

As my fitness improved, so did my cricket. Buckley's home ground was really small and was nicknamed the Postage Stamp but playing there made me really concentrate on nailing yorkers. Anything else would disappear for six, so it gave me some discipline with my bowling.

I started to create one or two headlines with my performances and I received a boost when I was invited to go and train with the Melbourne Stars Big Bash team, bowling in the nets to players like Russ, Kevin Pietersen and Luke Wright.

Another Notts teammate, Darren Pattinson, then arranged for me to practise with the Victoria state side. There was an outside chance that I might get a game as they were a bowler or two down but it didn't happen. That was a shame, as it would have been a real feather in my cap.

That winter in Australia was one of the best things I've ever done and apart from the cricket I'd learnt plenty of basic skills, washing, cooking and generally looking after myself most of the time, something I'd never had to do before.

I've been back to Australia to play for Buckley Ridges several times since and have always been looked after tremendously well by the 'Rattlers', Chris and his brother Tim.

Among the playing highlights of my time with Buckley Ridges have been a few personal moments to be proud of.

Twice I've top-scored in the T20 Grand Final for them. In January 2014 I hit 66 from only 20 deliveries against Berwick, scoring 48 from only nine balls, with three fours and six sixes.

The Berwick side included former Sri Lankan Test batsman Thilan Samaraweera, who had been injured during the Lahore terror attack some five years earlier.

My next Grand Final appearance was three years later and was another of my 'what if?' moments.

I scored 99 not out against Cranbourne, having been sent in at number three in the order, scoring the runs from only 38 balls in 49 minutes, an innings that included six fours and ten sixes, many of them disappearing either through or over the row of elm trees that lined the ground.

Starting the final over of our innings on 97, I only had myself to blame for not reaching three figures as I could only hit two singles from the last two balls I faced.

My bowling figures don't stack up too badly across the four seasons I've spent with the Melbourne club, taking a total of 112 wickets at an average of 13.21.

Among that haul was the least-celebrated hat-trick of all time, coming against a club called Coomoora. It had been spread over the course of two overs and no one realised until the scorers started shouting out.

Buckley Ridges has become a 'home from home' for Nottinghamshire players over the years. Apart from myself and Paul Franks, others to have made appearances for the Bucks include Alex Hales, David Hussey, Akhil Patel, Steven Mullaney, Harry Gurney and Tom Rowe, who spent time at the Notts academy.

Mullaney's stint was unfortunately cut short due to injury.

I've had some great times with him over the years but none finer than when we went to Australia together to play for Buckley Ridges. We'd both taken our families and everything was going well until his time was cut short due to a broken finger but I was able to share one memorable experience with him.

Our former teammate Darren Pattinson, brother of James, took us both out to Port Phillip Bay, off Melbourne, for a day's fishing.

It was a red hot day and we all got a touch of sunburn but we also caught plenty of fish. Patto knew of this spot, I'm not sure how, and we all had a rod each.

We must have caught 50 fish, I caught plenty of snapper but Mull had his moment of glory: 'I'd never been fishing in my life – not once. But went along anyway and thanks to Darren put a rod over the side. The very first fish I caught was a shark, a banjo shark.'

10

Stop That Bus

PART OF our prize for winning the championship had been an invitation to take part in the champion county match against MCC. Traditionally, this curtain-raiser to the new season had been held at Lord's but the previous year it had been moved to Abu Dhabi and had gone so well that MCC were keen to repeat it.

We were accommodated on Yas Island, the home of the Abu Dhabi Formula One Grand Prix, and everything was as opulent and expensive as you can imagine.

The Sheikh Zayed Stadium was virtually surrounded by nothing but desert back then but it didn't stop the fans coming out in their numbers to watch MCC practise.

Rahul Dravid, one of the top three Test match players in the world, had accepted an invitation to play for the MCC side, so the locals and many expat Indian supporters queued for photographs and autographs as the great man completed his net session.

As you'll read later on, I did manage to dismiss the man known as 'The Wall' in the first innings of that match but we were still heavily beaten inside three days.

It was the first time any of us had played a match using a pink ball, which was being trialled. We discovered that during normal daylight hours it didn't do anything, it was as flat as anything and you couldn't get it to move around at all.

But under lights, especially once the dew had come down, the ball nibbled and zipped around a bit.

We've since played a couple of County Championship matches with the pink ball but I dislike it, I'm not a fan of it at all.

I can remember using it in a county match at Trent Bridge against Kent, it was 9.30pm, no one was there and I was thinking, 'What am I doing here? I should be getting ready to be tucked up in bed and I've still got five overs to bowl.' Jeez.

The trialling of the pink ball went on for a number of years but I think it was all a process towards using it for Tests. Authorities seemed to think that everyone would rush back from work and watch day-night Tests or first-class cricket but they soon realised it was a pointless suggestion in England.

Tests are well supported here anyway and no one wanted to hang around until all hours at the championship matches it was used in. Hopefully, it has now been scrapped for good.

Mind you, perhaps I'm being a little harsh on the pink ball as I did manage to get eight wickets in the match – four in each innings – using it!

That match was played in March and it suited me perfectly, as I'd just returned from a full winter in Australia. Playing outdoors regularly, and bowling lots of overs, I had a huge advantage over many of the others.

I'd also returned from my winter away feeling fit and healthy, something that shocked Mick Newell: 'I wasn't with the Notts team for that trip, as I was away in the Caribbean on an England Lions tour.

'I couldn't quite believe it when I saw video footage of him bowling. He's certainly a person of extremes and to that point had never had a consistent lifestyle.

'He actually had lost a lot of weight and looked slim but I discovered that he'd done a lot of training in bin bags to get ready for the trip.'

At the end of our short tour to the UAE we faced a long final day, which involved travelling to Dubai to play in a T20 competition, then back to Abu Dhabi to take the night flight home.

The previous evening, ideally, should really have been spent in the hotel, packing and resting up, I suppose. If that had been a firm order then I'm sure we would have been happy to comply.

As it was, a handful of us went out for a quiet drink, which eventually turned into a massive one. A really, really massive one!

The coach was due to leave from outside our hotel at 9am on the final day. I was sharing a room with Jake Ball and I'm not sure what time either of us hit our beds but I was very much the worse for wear when the room telephone dragged me back into consciousness.

'Ugh,' I offered.

'Where the f**k are you?' It was Hales. 'We're all on the coach and it's ready to go.'

The conversation had woken Bally up and almost before I'd put the receiver down he was out of bed, had pulled his tracksuit on and was heading out of the door.

Such was his hurry, he left his watch and phone behind.

'Don't let it go without me,' I pleaded. But he was already out of earshot.

I knew I'd got a thumping hangover by this stage but was aware that we should have packed our things, so quickly threw everything into my suitcase for later.

Someone was obviously looking over me then because I made it downstairs and was surprised to see the coach still there. A car had pulled up in front of the coach and been randomly abandoned. The owner had presumably legged it into the hotel but now couldn't be found.

Those precious moments had saved me from being in real trouble, although I did get a good dressing down from Wayne Noon later on in the day. 'Don't do it if you can't hack it,' was the message. No need to listen, I'd heard it before.

The bus journey from Abu Dhabi to Dubai was interesting, one long highway cutting through the desert. Intermittently we'd see camels on either side of the road.

With our fuzzy heads having made a full recovery we enjoyed ourselves by winning the T20 competition in style, defeating MCC in the semi-final and Sussex in the final.

Our journey back towards Abu Dhabi was memorable for one incident. The driver just pulled over at one point, locked his coach and disappeared.

With the clock ticking towards our flight time, things became a little anxious on board. Where was he?

We were parked on the side of a dual carriageway, with our driver having disappeared into the one house in the distance.

At the behest of those in charge Hales kicked the centre door of the coach out and a search party set off.

Apparently, he was tucking into his dinner. His driving hours seemed to include a stop-off at his house for supper.

11

Warm Hearts, Hot Tongue

NOTTINGHAMSHIRE HAVE used Barbados as a pre-season training base many times during my time with the club.

What a beautiful island it is, a really lovely place to visit and the people are so friendly. I love their way of life and the fact they've all got a warm heart. It's just so good there.

Apart from the warm weather and the gorgeous sandy beaches, it's difficult to ignore the rich cricket history that Barbados possesses.

On our visits we have been extremely fortunate to meet some of the very best to have played the game, including Sir Garfield Sobers.

Sir G helped put Nottinghamshire on the global map, having played for the county between 1968 and 1974. Those fortunate enough to have seen him play during that period still talk about the aura of the man.

Meeting him and talking to him about his days at Trent Bridge has been one of the biggest highlights of my visits there.

Another former Nottinghamshire player, Franklyn Stephenson, has a cricket academy over there, which we've used as a training base on our visits. Franky has not only provided some of the best facilities for us to use, but also lays on some of the best barbecues.

Other first-class county sides have often been on the island when we've been there and we've been very fortunate to have played some of them in matches at the world-famous Kensington Oval.

It's also not the worst place to enjoy some down time and we've enjoyed fabulous golf days on the island at the world famous Sandy Lane course.

With so much on offer there's no wonder that occasionally I've enjoyed myself a little too much, as Wayne Noon recalls: 'One year we had told the players that they were going to have an appraisal on the last morning of the Barbados tour.

'Everyone was given their own time slot and made aware of the importance of being there on time.

'Fletch rocked up in the same clothes he'd gone out in the night before, presumably having only just returned from a lengthy night out.

'He really got it from Mick [Newell] then. Apart from anything else Fletch must have been so uncomfortable, it was so hot and he was still in his going-out gear.'

12

Mind That Car

DURING THE winter of 2014/15 I had the chance to go and play for Wellington Firebirds in New Zealand's domestic T20 tournament.

The opportunity came about after the Firebirds' captain, James Franklin, had spent time as a teammate of mine at Trent Bridge and had been suitably impressed by the accuracy of my death bowling.

He didn't need to twist my arm for long before I agreed to it. I could only see benefits. Having the chance to visit a new country and to play cricket there was something that excited me.

Even better, I discovered that the tournament was being sponsored by a local pie company and was magnificently entitled The Georgie Pie Super Smash.

Apart from James, our team had a few other guys that I'd met before, including Warwickshire spinner Jeetan Patel and the Australian international Brad Hodge, who was the other overseas player allowed.

Flying around New Zealand, in order to visit and play in the different cities, was a great experience, although it had its drawbacks, as I quickly discovered.

Leaving Wellington invariably meant that at some point we would have to return, giving me a stomach-churning and very graphic explanation as to how the city earned its nickname.

One journey will stay with me for the rest of my life. We had been playing somewhere and were flying back to our home base.

As usual I was sat with Grant Elliott (I remember how alphabetically structured everything was there; E – Elliott and F – Fletcher – can go next to each other).

We were on this diddy little plane and it was starting to blow outside. Grant said, 'Now you're going to see why it's called "The Windy City".'

The plane was swirling around, erratically being thrown from side to side. I was properly sh****ng myself and was so relieved when we landed.

The tournament itself took some getting used to. Every game was televised live across the nation but attendances within the grounds were small, only ranging from around 500 to 1,000.

One incident that happened has gained a spot of notoriety. We were in Hamilton playing Otago at Seddon Park and I found myself bowling to Jesse Ryder, the hard-hitting Kiwi international.

The powerful left-hander is a typical T20 specialist, who goes as hard as he can in the opening powerplay and on this particular day he hit 56 from only 25 balls.

My first delivery to him was full and in a decent area but he had got his eye in and pulled it high over midwicket and out of the ground for six.

The reason it has been shown time and time again and attracted a colossal amount of online attention is because of the commentary.

Broadcaster Ian Smith, the former Test wicketkeeper, was behind the microphone and during the flight of the ball his tone suddenly changed.

From gushing about the powerful blow, he quickly went into panic mode as he realised the ball had sailed into the parking area and struck his car, badly denting the roof.

Everyone still takes the mickey out of me for being on the receiving end of that mighty Ryder hit but it wasn't that bad an over in truth and only cost me a total of seven runs, despite that blow. And we went on to win the match!

It was a privilege to play at some wonderful venues during that tournament. Eden Park in Auckland stands out as an incredible ground and I couldn't have wished to make a better start to a match than I did on my first appearance there.

Martin Guptill, another high-quality international cricketer, nicked my first ball behind and then Rob Nicol followed a few deliveries later, giving me one of only two occasions when I've sent down a double-wicket maiden in a T20.

Things were going well for me individually during a hectic run of matches but that's usually the time when my fortunes change and they did so on this occasion.

Prior to a home match at the wonderful Westpac Stadium, known locally as the Cake Tin, I had spent some time practising my batting at the Basin Reserve, the other major stadium in the city.

I did a bit of 'range hitting', just basically whacking the ball as far as I could. There was a twinge in my side after one enormous hit but I shrugged it off as nothing to worry about.

It stiffened overnight but I still felt fit enough to play, on what was a typically gusty Wellington day.

Running in to bowl I was being buffeted around by the blustery conditions. As I released the ball I felt a sharp pain in my side. I was unable to continue and feared the worst. The diagnosis was devastating, I'd torn my side and was immediately ruled out of the rest of the tournament.

My Super Smash was over but there was some slight compensation in that, even without me, the Firebirds went on to win the final.

Cricket has also taken me to India and Oman for training camps and to Potchefstroom in South Africa for a pre-season tour with Notts.

13

Windows Of Opportunity

I LIKE structure in my life. Tell me when and where you want me, give me a schedule and I'm happy.

The county cricket season is ideal, therefore, for someone like me. Out come the fixtures, we know where we're going and when and barring one or two runs to the knockout stages of white-ball competitions our year is clearly mapped out for us.

That doesn't mean to say things always run smoothly, of course. Injuries, squad rotation and being unexpectedly out of favour can all create a spot of mayhem and uncertainty but normally life follows a familiar pattern for your county pro.

A new calendar year will usually find most players in decent physical fitness. By then they will have been back in regular training for a couple of months.

Personally, January is usually pretty tough for me.

It's a medical condition I have which comes around every year at Yuletide – it's commonly known as 'pigs in blankets', I believe, although there's plenty of other tasty goodies around which I similarly find difficult to resist. I've always enjoyed a good Christmas and tend to tuck in.

As a result of my indulgences the first two or three months of a new year are always very hard for me but I know there's a purpose to life, a reason to get up in the morning.

The cricket season is just around the corner and I know that I have to get myself ready. I've never taken it for granted that I would be an automatic selection for Notts but I have always tried to give myself the best chance of being picked.

Anyone who has spent that period with me will know how much I throw myself into it.

To be totally honest – and this may not surprise you – fitness has always been something of an issue for me so I have to commit to it.

What I will say is, and I'd hope every coach I've ever played under would agree, I've never slacked and always given 100 per cent in training.

Old-school me would tell everyone that I trained on Estrella, peanuts, garlic bread and s**t like that.

But the reality is different.

Whatever the strength and conditioning coaches throw in my direction I try to embrace, whether it's running, swimming, cycling, circuit training, team bonding exercises, protein shakes or anything else.

I know it has to be done, so I just get on and do it. And I do it because I love cricket so much.

There are elements of the pre-season fitness training that I prefer more than others, obviously.

Every year we have a gruelling run to complete, I'm not sure if it's right to call it a cross-country run as it's almost exclusively uphill.

It's done at a place called Gotham – no, not the *Batman* one – and people ask me how steep this hill is. I tell them that it's so high at the top that we have to duck underneath the aeroplanes as they come in to land at East Midlands airport.

Every winter you know that the Gotham Hill run is coming but don't know exactly when it will happen, you only find out the day before.

It's a killer and myself and Samit Patel are usually lagging near the back but at least we know what it entails. Our fun is usually found at the expense of others, especially those that are new to the club and experiencing it for the first time.

No names – but I'm not sure they have anything to rival it at a county in the north-west!

My forte, believe it or not, comes in the triathlon. Never judge a book by the cover, they say.

We do a 5km run, 40 lengths of the swimming pool and then a further 30km on the bike and it's been a source of personal pride that I've managed to have a lengthy spell of winning that particular activity.

My struggle has always been with maintenance, I'm either up or down. Even as a kid, my mum used to say that I was 'in and out the doors like a yo-yo'. Nothing has changed.

The only thing that is consistent in my life is my bowling. Everything else is all over the shop.

But I live like that so that I can enjoy my season.

There are people in all walks of life that live to work, I'd like to think that it's the other way round with me, I work to live.

While I have always been a big lad it should be clear to anyone that I've had to maintain a certain level of fitness to do what I do.

There's a big amount of stress running through my body with every delivery I send down but I've always bowled my overs and never shirked anything, either on the pitch or in training.

I've rarely been out injured either, whereas some of the lads with six packs have often been unavailable for this niggle or that.

What works for me might be different for someone else, of course. Take Samit for example.

Everyone goes on about him for his fitness but he's the only cricketer I know who has never missed a game through injury in his whole career. That's quite remarkable, I'm sure you'll agree.

It's an unbelievable stat for someone who has the fitness coaches pulling their hair out. Fair play to him, he plays every single game.

My preparation for the new season will have begun in earnest once the fixtures are released. Usually out the previous November, the closer we get to April the more I scrutinise them.

Early season matches at Trent Bridge always attract my attention as it tends to do a bit there early on, especially when it's green.

It's important for everyone to start a new campaign well and I'm no different. Cricket is a team sport and 100 per cent I want my team to be doing well but it's also important to make a contribution yourself.

In a stat-driven industry the figures are important. People will look at bowlers and scrutinise. Wickets, averages, economy rates.

Despite telling you how much I like structure in my life, I do also get bored with routine and need letting off the leash occasionally.

I do enjoy the odd spontaneous event. A window of opportunity, I call it.

Mick Newell always used to say about me, 'Fletch is a person of extremes and has never had a consistent lifestyle. He doesn't do a quiet drink. It's either a noisy one or no drink at all.'

He's right, of course. At times in the past I've got some of my 'windows of opportunity' terribly wrong and I'd be the first to hold my hands up and admit it.

Nowadays I try and pick the right moment.

I still need that occasional release, so I can re-start another chapter of routine.

14

The Great BT

I ENJOYED the three years that Brendan Taylor (BT) spent with us at Notts. He'd had a stellar international career with Zimbabwe, which had culminated in some outrageous performances at the 2015 ICC World Cup, where he averaged over 72 with the bat. He opened his account with us by scoring hundreds in his first two matches but apart from his undoubted quality I loved his attitude to life and his infectious laughter.

We clicked and became good buddies, so it's no surprise that we got into one or two scrapes.

* * *

Brendan Taylor: 'During my time at Notts, whenever my family were away, I would go round to Fletch's and we would watch a movie and get some food delivered.

'We were both very partial to a Papa John's pizza, complete with extra chillies. I'd always look over at him and be astonished at how quickly he'd eat his food, he almost inhaled it.

'It became a bit of a competition with him to see how fast he could demolish a pizza; he was always determined to finish his the quickest.

'One day, even as he was opening the box, he began thrashing slices of it down his neck, stuffing it in as lava-hot cheese flicked around his mouth and stuck to his neck. It was just the funniest thing to see him trying to scratch it off before it burnt him.

'He almost got third degree burns as he stuffed it in and was panting like a dog at the heat of the chillies. I think he had to wash it all down with a litre of orangeade.

'Fletch always had a big night in him but I think he's changed a little since becoming a family man. Those memories will live with me forever, though.'

* * *

BT has other memories to look back on from his time in Nottingham, noticeably the infamous occasion when he upset one of his neighbours.

My name got dragged into it, typically, but for once I was only on the periphery of the actual incident.

We had pulled off a pretty decent win over Durham in a day-night one-day match at Trent Bridge. It had gone on until very late in the evening after a rain delay and we were jubilant to come through it.

A quiet celebration turned into a visit to a casino and then into headline-making news, which BT would love to forget about.

* * *

Brendan Taylor: 'That incident was fuelled by Fletch, not that I needed much encouragement. We'd had a great win and there was a party mood in the changing rooms, with Fletch kicking it off with a few beers.

'We went pretty hard at it and then decided to go out into town for some more. I made the fatal error of not eating, whereas Fletch ticked that box by scoffing down a McDonald's to line his stomach.

'I know we went to the casino but the rest of the night is a bit of a blur but it transpired that Samit had taken me home in a taxi. He wasn't sure which house I lived at, so dropped me off in the middle of my road.

'It was raining pretty hard and seemingly, I couldn't find my house either but I discovered a car that had been left unlocked, climbed in and fell asleep.

'It hadn't been my car.

'The next morning a guy had gone to his car, seen me, and had called the police.

'I was very apologetic and it was all sorted out fairly amicably with a couple of bottles of wine and some tickets for him and his family.

'It was something I was obviously very embarrassed about but I'm glad everyone took it the right way.

'I'd like to be remembered for one or two performances from my Notts days but that episode seems to trump it all, so I have to take it on the chin and accept it.'

* * *

Poor old BT. If things hadn't been bad enough, the newspapers got hold of the story and had a field day at his expense.

The first time I discovered something had been wrong was when Brendan's wife, Kelly, had called me at breakfast time, wondering where her husband was (presumably he was still outside asleep in the car at that time).

I did what any concerned mate would do – denied all knowledge and suggested she ring Samit!

Soon afterwards we had a four-day match away at Edgbaston against Warwickshire. The football fixtures had been kind because on the second or third evening Nottingham Forest were also in town, playing Birmingham City at St Andrew's.

Tickets were sorted out and a few of us went down – myself, Brendan, Samit, Alex Hales and Jake Ball.

We were right in the middle of the Forest fans and as usual they'd travelled in big numbers.

During the second half word obviously spread that we were there among them and a song started up, 'He sleeps where he wants, he sleeps where he wants, Brendan Taylor, he sleeps where he wants.'

To hear five or six thousand Forest fans giving it to our favourite Zimbabwean was just brilliant.

BT just happened to be there on the occasion that I did that charity night in which Alex turned up unexpectedly.

* * *

Brendan Taylor: 'Whenever Fletch has a night out you can guarantee that a few people will tag along and it will be fun. I don't think even he expected so many to turn up when he announced he was doing that Q and A.

'Myself and one or two of the other players decided to show him some support and went along. It was unbelievable. Fletch had downed a few pints and a couple of Jagerbombs for Dutch courage and was on top form.

'As I looked around the room I could see almost 200 people crying with laughter. The big lad was in his element and it's a hell of a skill to be able to make people laugh like that.

'I had stomach cramps from laughing at him and for Alex to drive over and say, "I'm not going to miss this for the world," shows how much humour he has and how well loved he is, not just in Nottingham but everywhere else also.

'Fletch is clearly the most popular guy in county cricket.'

* * *

The campaign that we've had defines how hard we hit the end-of-season drinks. If we've had a bit of a shocker it's only natural that our supporters wouldn't want to see us out celebrating but if we've had a good year, then it can be a bit chaotic.

Take 2017, for example, when we won both of the white-ball competitions and also achieved promotion back to the top flight.

Following the final match of the season we'll have a massive fines meeting in the dressing room. If we've played at home then we'll just get on with it or if we're away then it may wait until the next day.

Club cricketers will all have experienced something similar at the end of their seasons, I'm sure. Fines will be imposed for all sorts of misdemeanours that have occurred over the season – and very often have been prone to huge exaggeration.

Experience teaches you that it's always best to shut up and pay up and not try and argue your case.

It's all done in good humour, knowing that the kitty will then be blown a day or two later on the annual tram crawl.

Nottingham is well known for its excellent tram service, running from the outer suburbs right into the city centre.

The plan is always to make our way out to the end of the line at Hucknall and then get off at each stop and have a drink on the way back in.

One of the first stops is at Bulwell, my home town, where we always encounter one or two rogues. All know me, or claim to, of course, and the rest of the lads will have plenty of fun at my expense.

I've omitted to mention that this is all done while wearing fancy dress. A lot of thought goes into the costume and from about July onwards you'll hear players whispering about it or notice them trawling through fancy dress websites.

I'll never forget the year that Samit Patel knocked us all dead when he turned up as a Power Ranger.

My favourite ever costume was cruelly sabotaged by Brendan Taylor, something he still finds funny.

* * *

Brendan Taylor: 'The tram crawl was one of the highlights of my time at Notts. We were split into groups beforehand and secretively bought our outfits online.

'One year my group all dressed as Alan, the guy with the beard out of *The Hangover*. Fletch's group were all Ghostbusters.

'As you can imagine, his was quite a big suit and came with a battery-operated back pack that blew it up. It made Fletch look like a kid that had been swallowed by the Michelin Man!

'Outside a pub I borrowed a cigarette off someone and popped a few holes in his battery pack. It was like popping bubble wrap.

'Chris Read saw me doing it and was killing himself laughing, properly enjoying it but Fletch didn't know what was going off at first until he realised his suit was shrinking.'

* * *

I loved that outfit!

Very often we'll wave goodbye to one or two players at the end of the tram crawl, with some of the lads either leaving the club or others going off to catch flights for a winter abroad.

Those who remain behind will have a further couple of events to attend to; the official club end-of-season awards night and the Professional Cricketers' Association (PCA) do.

I consider myself to be very proud and very fortunate to have won a few Nottinghamshire awards over the years. I've loved every single second of my time with the county and have always tried to do my best, so when some recognition does come along, even a big daft lad like me can get emotional.

Usually the next day we'll all meet at Hooters for a livener before going down to the train station together for the PCA do in London.

Once that is all done and dusted it's almost time for some down time and depending on your circumstances, it may be time for a break overseas.

Now, as a family man, things tends to be a little quieter for me than in the past but there have been some stand-out trips over the years.

On one occasion I managed to get away for a few days immediately after the last match, heading off to Ibiza with some mates and my brother for three or four days.

It was totally random and I couldn't wait for the match to finish. The final afternoon of the match was spent at square leg chatting to umpire Nigel Llong and repeatedly telling him how much I wanted the captains to agree to an early handshake and get the match over, so I could get away to the airport.

Another year I went to Las Vegas with a few of the lads, including Hales. Any stories from that trip are strictly embargoed, though. You know the saying, 'What happens in Vegas stays in Vegas!'

15

Through Thick And Thin

IF YOU are fortunate enough to stay at one particular county over a number of years then inevitably you move up the pecking order in terms of seniority.

With that not only comes extra responsibility but also new teammates to get to know and appreciate.

It didn't take very long for the first Nottinghamshire sides I played in to be transformed almost totally.

Experienced players such as Ryan Sidebottom, Graeme Swann, Mark Ealham, Ali Brown, Mark Wagh, Charlie Shreck and Andre Adams – plus many others of course – made way for a younger brigade.

Chris Read and Samit Patel were constants across all three formats and had been joined in the team by Steven Mullaney, Jake Ball and Harry Gurney as we searched for success.

Mull had joined us from Lancashire ahead of the 2010 season and had played a major role in our title win.

Good enough to captain the England Lions on a few occasions, he was the heir apparent to take over when Chris Read eventually stood down.

* * *

Steven Mullaney: 'I've got on with Fletch since the first day I signed for Notts. Him, Hales and Andy Carter met me and took me out for a curry.

'Since then I've always thought of him as a good mate and he's a real pleasure to be around. He's also a very good cricketer and one of the hardest workers at the club. No one can ever question his commitment to Notts.

'What he does well is, he gets the best batsmen out. You look at his first-class record and you can see all the big names are on there.

'He's been very economical over the years because everyone gives him the greatest respect when he's bowling but when he pushes the ball right up there he's particularly dangerous. I just wonder if the time will come when he starts to go for a few more runs as he looks to get the ball right up there to find a few more edges.'

* * *

Harry Gurney came to us down that well-trodden track from Leicestershire. The first time I met him properly he was sat up in our changing room when we came off the field for a lunch break.

I knew who he was as I'd recently played against him in a second team match. Out of his earshot, I asked one or two of the lads, 'What's that Leicester seconds player doing here?'

It quickly got around that he'd come to sign a contract.

It all turned out pretty well though, didn't it? He's been unbelievable for us over the years and others haven't been slow to recognise his talents.

England recognition came his way fairly quickly but then disappeared again and it is a measure of his character and ability that he has fought back to become one of the best white-ball bowlers in world cricket.

'H' has made appearances in every top T20 competition throughout the world and has had an unbelievable run of winning titles right across the globe.

As a member of the fast-bowling cartel at Notts, we've shared some good times together.

* * *

Harry Gurney: 'It's difficult to explain how passionate Fletch is about his home city, he absolutely loves the place.

'He's become a proper Notts legend and the whole back story, where he came from, working at Hooters and all that, it just adds to his legendary status.

'His actual ability gets easily overlooked because of the way he's perceived but it shouldn't be, he's won countless awards and been our Player of the Year and deservedly so, because he is such a consistent performer.

'I think that gets overlooked because he's played in sides with the likes of Andre [Adams], Broady and Patto and it's easy for the focus to be on them and not Fletch.

'In my time at the club he's bowled some unbelievable spells for Notts but one of his greatest assets has been to get wickets when we've most needed it.

'The opposition can be 300/3, you're all stiff and knackered and he'll still find a way to nick someone off.

'And I've not even mentioned his T20 bowling – he must be up among the best yorker bowlers in the world.'

* * *

Jake Ball came through the academy system at Notts and I know how proud he is to represent his home county. Jake comes from good cricketing stock, most of the family are involved one way or another and his uncle is none other than former Notts and England wicketkeeper Bruce French.

The family ties to his home club, Welbeck, are even stronger now, as Notts have played a few matches there in the last few years, using the picturesque north Nottinghamshire venue as an out-ground.

Jake remembers the first one, in 2015: 'Fletch was bowling to Chris Woakes and let out a huge appeal for caught behind. The umpire was Peter Hartley and he gave it not out.

'It looked like Fletch was up for discussing it further and he turned to Woakes and said, "Did you nick it?"

'"No."

'That was good enough for Fletch, "All right, I'll believe you, cos you're a good lad."

'As he walked back past the umpire he let him know he was in his thoughts too, "And you're a good lad."

'But then he made us all laugh by turning to non-striker Ian Bell and said, "I'm not sure about you though!"

'That's how he is. Always something unexpected, always something to make us laugh.

'There are days when the pressure is on but Fletch has a way of cutting through that.

'He's an emotional man, when he's up everyone loves him and it's generally regarded that he's the most popular bloke on the circuit.

'If we are playing at Trent Bridge and it's mid-afternoon, a bit quiet and not much is happening, then he'll come alive.

'He will go down to the Radcliffe Road end and start waving his arms and shouting at them, "Come on then!"

'It gives everyone a lift and often leads to us getting a breakthrough and turning a match around.

'Freddie Flintoff loves him and it's easy to understand why.

'Fletch has a Flintoff impression that he does when he's bowling, trying to run in and deliver it like the great man used to do. He's done it a whole over before now and gets an extra bit of zip when he does it, as well.

'He's not renowned for being the brightest but perhaps he is after all, he's sharp as a tack when it comes to wit and making people laugh and I'm so happy to have played all my first-class cricket with him.'

I'd lived with Jake for a while at Gamston, a neighbourhood that was bursting with Nottinghamshire players at the time. He remembers a daily ritual that we had: 'Fletch lived with me around 2013/14 time and was actually a really good housemate. Mind you, we'd both previously experienced time living with Hales!

'Mull [Steven Mullaney] lived just around the corner and both Graeme White and Sam Wood lived nearby as well.

'We had a WhatsApp group between the five of us, called "Who's Going?"

'Whoever was last on there each evening had to go and fetch McFlurries for everyone else.'

16

Lord's Final 2017

ASK ANY youngster who enjoys football and they'll tell you that they dream of playing in an FA Cup final at Wembley.

Cricket's equivalent is a one-day final at Lord's and we're all the same. It is something that every cricketer – particularly those, like me, who don't experience the elation of international honours – yearns for.

Opportunities are limited, of course. In past years there would be two limited-overs competitions, two chances to get to Lord's. The introduction of T20 to our domestic calendar replaced one of the knockouts and now it seems as if the sole remaining final will be held away from Lord's each year.

In 2013 I didn't play in many of the group matches, so it wasn't really a surprise when I wasn't selected for our Lord's final against Glamorgan.

Four years later it was different. I'd played in most of the matches and can still remember vividly how excited I had felt when Peter Moores told me that I was going to play in the final.

I'm not one to reflect too deeply into things but on the eve of the match I kept thinking about how many balls I'd bowled in nets, practices and competitive matches since starting the game as a youngster. It was all for moments like this.

Constantly going through my mind was the thought that this was going to be the biggest day of my life, or certainly the biggest day of my cricketing career.

We'd gone down to our London hotel ahead of the big day and had a good practice session before going out to relax and take some fuel on board.

Several of us, including Harry Gurney, Steven Mullaney, Brendan Taylor and Jake Ball, went out for a meal to YO! Sushi, even though I don't really like sushi.

My personal plans were then to watch *Love Island* and get my head down at around ten o'clock. Off went the telly but I was far too excited for sleep and couldn't settle.

After hours of tossing and turning and several sessions of catching up with Twitter – which saw the clock tick slowly around from 2am to 3am – I started to panic, which obviously made things worse.

Eventually I managed to drift off and get a few hours of rest before the alarm startled me back into life. The sudden realisation of what was ahead hit me.

Like a young kid at Christmas I couldn't wait for the day's events to unfold and felt even better after an invigorating shower. I made my way down for breakfast but those that know me will be staggered by the next sentence.

It was the first time I can recall going down to tackle a breakfast buffet but being unable to eat much (I think I just settled for four sausages)!

For those of you who know Lord's and its geography you will be aware of the Danubius Hotel, which has a nice position overlooking the Nursery ground.

It's very close by and only really involves crossing the St John's Wood Road but I wanted to do it on my own and enjoy the stroll in.

There were one or two well-wishers around and the Lord's stewards, in their pristine white jackets, offered their usual polite greetings. A few of the players were already in the dressing room, going about their own preparations for the day.

I sought out Chris Read and said to the skipper, 'If we win the toss and bowl, please let me bowl the first ball of a Lord's final.'

Considering we'd got other options, such as Stuart Broad, Harry Gurney and James Pattinson, I was more than a little surprised when he nodded in agreement, 'Yeah, all right mate.'

* * *

Chris Read: 'From my point of view it wasn't a gamble. It was an overcast morning, so if anyone was going to get any movement it would be Fletch. We had good bowling resources but it wasn't a tough decision.

'To get the best out of Fletch he needs to bowl in either of two phases, the start of an innings and the end. He gets his lengths right then.

'He was always pretty easy to manage, just tell him what to do and he'll do it; it's either, "Take the new ball and stick it in good areas" or "it's the last 12 balls, so stick it in the hole".'

* * *

As it happened we lost the toss but Surrey's Gareth Batty opted to bat first anyway. So, on a glorious July morning we took to the field for the opening salvo of the final.

I knew what was coming as the captain huddled us all together on the edge of the outfield but I wonder if one or two of my teammates were a little taken aback as he announced, 'Fletch, take the first over from the pavilion end.'

Our one-day results had improved dramatically since losing our opening two group games but we only just squeaked out of our group.

Billy Root's hundred at Edgbaston had given us a much-needed victory over Warwickshire but it took a heavy downpour at Northampton in our final match to confirm our place in the knockouts.

To reach Lord's we would have to win two tough away matches but we played almost perfect cricket in both of them.

We'd gone to Taunton first of all, to face one of our bogey sides, Somerset. Michael Lumb had helped to get us off to a rattling start and with Brendan Taylor playing his best innings in a Notts shirt we scored 429/9.

The Cidermen are always tough opponents, particularly on their own patch, and this turned into a crazy match. They certainly had us worried for a while before coming up short at 405 all out.

Next it was Essex in front of a partisan Chelmsford crowd. Hundreds from Alastair Cook and Ryan ten Doeschate had set us a huge target of 371 but our confidence was sky-high at that time and centuries from Samit Patel and Steven Mullaney had seen us through.

The only side that could now prevent us taking the silverware back to Nottingham were Surrey, who had easily defeated Worcestershire in the other semi to reach their third consecutive final.

Jason Roy, the hard-hitting England international, had scored 92 for the London side in their victory at New Road and walked down to the business end to take the first ball of the final.

I was more than aware that it was very important for me to set the right tone and begin with an accurate opening over.

A wave of emotion swept over me as I waited for umpire Tim Robinson to call 'play'. I'd bowled thousands and thousands of deliveries and this, in isolation, should be no different – but of course it was.

The enormity of the occasion couldn't be put aside. Lord's wasn't completely packed to the rafters but there was a fairly healthy crowd and the Nottinghamshire supporters were making lots of noise from their perches in the Compton Stand.

Walking to my mark, ahead of the opening delivery, I glanced around. The seating areas of the pavilion contained plenty of members attired in their egg and bacon colours. Who would the neutrals among them be rooting for, the London side or the team from the Midlands?

At the other end of the ground the iconic Media Centre appeared to be jammed full of journalists, broadcasters and commentators.

Many of whom would be concentrating on me right now, 'Here comes Fletcher to bowl the opening delivery of the final.'

In I ran, determined to put the ball in a good area, just outside off stump. Jason Roy pushed at it timidly as it nibbled away from him. The ball kissed the outside edge and flew gently towards first slip, where Riki Wessels was waiting.

Wessels had spent much of his career as a wicketkeeper but after arriving at Trent Bridge he had quickly accepted that his role would be as a front-line batsman and someone who could take over the gloves in an emergency if anything had ever happened to Chris Read.

Over the previous three or four seasons he had shown himself to be an outstanding slip catcher, pulling off some amazing dismissals in that time.

As the ball made its way towards him I had no concerns that he would catch it. This was one he'd take at least nine times of ten.

Inexplicably, this was the one occasion when he didn't hang on. The ball was dropping all the time and he went to take it round about knee height but somehow it burst through his hands and ran away for a single.

All those positive thoughts about setting the right tone for the day and getting off to a solid start had vanished in an instant.

* * *

Chris Read: 'The first ball landed in exactly the right spot and I remember thinking "Hallelujah", then down it went.

'The first ball had been right on the money and we'd missed a chance and seemed to take it badly collectively. You could see our heads drop at the disappointment.'

* * *

It's difficult to describe what comes over a side in a moment like that. Dropped catches don't just affect the culprit. Individually, every one of us knew that we'd missed a golden opportunity to remove a very dangerous player and put Surrey on the back foot.

Collectively we were poor over the next hour, leaking a succession of boundaries. I was taken off after going for about 25 in three overs.

Was it nerves? I'm not sure but the television commentators – I later discovered – felt we'd erred by bowling on both sides of the wicket. I can't argue with their assessment.

A couple of other chances went down that we'd normally take and we weren't helping ourselves in the field either, generally pretty sloppy in our ground work.

Dark thoughts were already forming. I began to have a feeling of foreboding.

I'd had a sense of what this day could have been for me but it was now beginning to turn the other way. What a hero I'd have been if I'd taken a wicket first ball and what might have happened then?

Kumar Sangakkara, one of the best players in the world, would have been coming out to face just the second ball of the final.

Negative thoughts shouldn't start to have an impact but it did cross my mind that playing in a Lord's final might well turn out to be my only highlight of the day.

Gradually though, things started to happen for us. Samit and Mull, as they'd done so many times when bowling in tandem, got us back in it and shared the first five wickets to fall as we pegged Surrey back to 180/5.

We were fighting hard and I was able to contribute when I was brought back on in the later stages. I managed to bowl Gareth Batty with a straight one and bellowed out a roar of satisfaction as the stumps were hit.

My celebrations were of relief, as much as anything, and included a salute towards the Tavern Stand, where Kirsty, my parents, Sam, and his partner Liz, were sat.

Mark Stoneman batted right through their innings, scoring an unbeaten 144, but their eventual total of 297/9 could have been so much worse for us. I closed with bowling figures of 1-37.

During the interval I thought this was very much game on and sensed that the rest of the dressing room were optimistic about our chances.

Now it was the time for our batsmen to deliver but we had a huge scare early on when Ollie Pope put down a simple chance in the covers off Alex Hales.

I needed to find a good vantage point to watch the action from and headed for the baths. Hoping not to be needed, Harry Gurney and I remained there for about two and a half hours, having a good soak while watching our innings unfold.

Hales was brilliant but no one could stay with him for long enough to ease our anxieties. It was becoming increasingly clear that if we were going to win this final then two things needed to happen.

Our hard-hitting opener was going to have to be there at the end and he was going to need some proper support from the lower order.

As you've already discovered, Baz and I go a long way back and I always knew he had this sort of performance in him.

This was his stage. Many have described it as the best one-day innings they've seen and I wouldn't argue with them, as he refused to be tied down, cutting, driving and improvising against everything that Surrey threw at him.

Chris Read, signing off before retirement at the end of the season, had made a name for himself by always chipping in with runs when they were needed. Once again, our captain delivered, joining Hales in a stand of 137 to almost take us over the line.

During our long soak in the bath I'd noticed that Surrey's seamers were getting the ball to reverse nicely, so when I made it back out on to the balcony I couldn't resist having a bit of fun with one of them.

Tom Curran was fielding on the rope in front of us, so I yelled, 'Hey Tom, we're watching you on the telly mate, mind what your fingers are doing with that ball.'

He went ballistic, firing some industrial language back in my direction. Quite what the members thought of it, I'm not sure!

In many ways his response was understandable because they knew the match was lost by then.

It was a real shame that our skipper couldn't be there at the end but Readie was dismissed with just a handful of runs needed and received one of the best ovations I've ever heard as he left the big stage for the final time.

James Pattinson went out and confidently stroked the winning runs and that was that, we'd won the Royal London One-Day Cup Final.

Of course, it was chiefly down to Hales that we'd done it. His unbeaten 187 will live long in the memory and will take some beating as the highest individual score in a Lord's final.

Unless you are extremely fortunate – or named Mo Farah, or Lionel Messi or something – you will experience more down days than good days in professional sport.

So when the good times do roll around it's important to make the most of them. The few hours after that winning run had been hit will stay with me forever, although they began rather strangely.

Several of us had already been presented with our medals when someone noticed the inscription on the back, 'Womens One-Day Cup Champions 2017'.

The organisers had brought the wrong medals to the presentation ceremony but promises were made to get them exchanged at a later date.

No one cared really. All we wanted to do was get down to the far end of the ground and celebrate with our supporters. They had been fantastic throughout the day, waving their flags and cheering us on, so we were glad to give them something to remember.

Joyous scenes followed as we caught up with family members and friends. It was the first time that my mum and dad had been to Lord's and they'd had a fabulous time, drinking champagne and joining in with the singing.

It was great to catch up with them and share some emotional moments before heading back to the dressing room to properly celebrate the win.

The Surrey team joined us for a while and couldn't have been more gracious – a top bunch of lads who put aside their own disappointment to warmly congratulate us.

It's a good job everyone was in such a happy mood because I nearly got myself in it, as usual. There had been so many bottles of champers knocking around that I had poured some over the heads of one or two of the backroom staff and club media.

Then I noticed another full bottle or two and did the same – big mistake, as I quickly discovered.

Lisa Pursehouse, our chief executive, had brought in some Special Edition Lord's Champagne, at £200 a bottle, to toast us.

Time to keep my head down!

We were eventually thrown out of the ground at around 10.30pm and went back to the hotel to continue the revelry.

Without doubt, it had been an incredible day, the highlight of my career. I'm so glad I experienced it – because you never know what might be just around the corner!

Hello there!

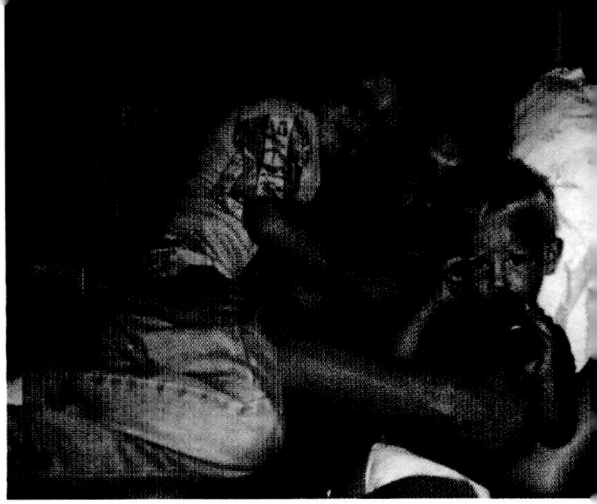

I'm on the right here, two years younger than Tom and two years older than Sam. This was taken on a caravan holiday at Chapel St. Leonards.

The three of us relaxing with Dad, I'm in the middle

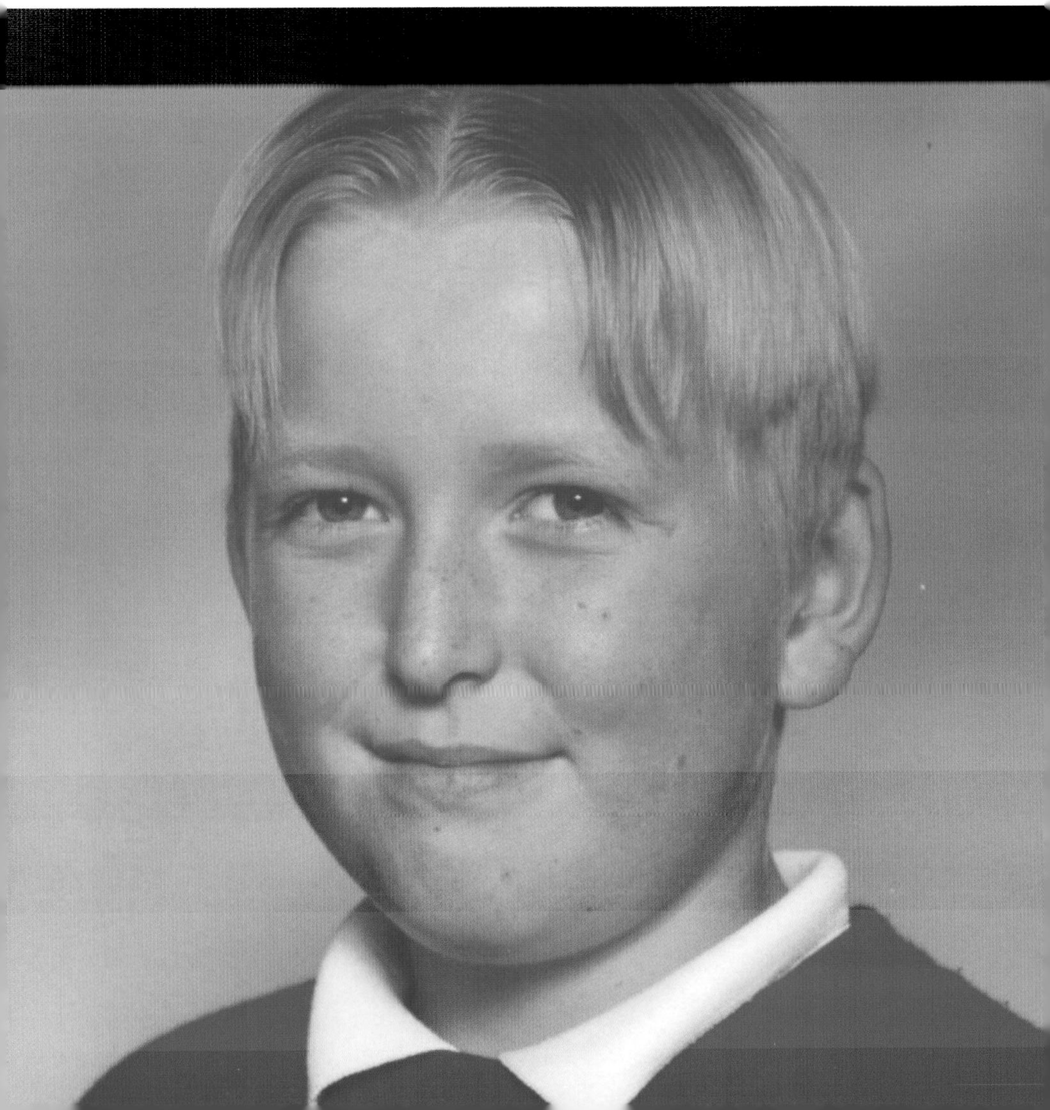

Cantrell Primary School before our match at Old Trafford

Playing in goal at Wembley Stadium for Nottingham City Boys and (right) being introduced on the pitch to former England goalkeeper Peter Shilton

Thank you Santa, my first cricket kit

A favourite photo with Mum. Both parents have been so supportive throughout my career

Nothing too scientific about my shirt number – I was 19 years old when I signed my first contract

In South Africa with Mark Wagh (left) and Mick Newell on my first overseas trip with Notts

On England Under-19 duty

Hitting out on the way to making 92 against Hampshire

2010 County Championship winning celebrations

A title winner in my first full year and to share the experience with my mate Baz was just unbelievable

Hitting towards that short boundary on my way to an unbeaten 99 in a cup final

Building up a thirst

I've had some great times playing for Buckley Ridges in Australia

Lining up for a T20 final at the mighty MCG

17

Contrasting Emotions

OUR LORD'S success had taken place on Saturday, 1 July 2017 and we partied hard for a couple of days before getting back to business.

We had won the first piece of silverware available and still had hopes of completing a domestic treble. Following County Championship relegation the previous season, we had been installed as firm favourites for an immediate return and had made a positive start to the red-ball campaign.

Now it was time to switch our focus to the shortest format, the T20 competition. Our record over the years had been good, to a certain extent, with a succession of quarter-final appearances. But we still hadn't lifted the crown.

Fresh from our Lord's success we knew this could be our year. We had players in form and were high on confidence.

Three or four good days of practice set us up nicely for our first match, at Headingley against Yorkshire.

The nature of T20 is that you can always be vulnerable if someone comes off and plays a special innings. On that particular evening, opener Adam Lyth and Shaun Marsh, the Australian Test player, middled everything they faced and we were well beaten.

Not the best of starts but with 14 matches to play in the group it wasn't anything to get too concerned about, especially as 24 hours later we were to be back in action, at Edgbaston against the Birmingham Bears.

On 8 July at around 7pm we started our match against the Bears. It was almost exactly one week on from us lifting the Royal London One-Day Cup at Lord's.

In front of the television cameras we were looking to put on a show and get the Yorkshire loss out of our system.

The omens weren't great as we struggled to 28/3 within the first four overs, losing Hales, Lumb and Wessels.

Thanks to 55 from Samit we recovered to 158/6 but it was a score that meant we were always going to be under pressure.

Birmingham opened with Ian Bell and Sam Hain and the pair crashed 30 runs off the first two overs; at which point I got the nod to bowl the third.

I knew that both batsmen would be looking to come hard at me and try and make the most of the powerplay overs.

Hain was facing and I looked to bowl the first one towards middle and leg and not give him any room, so I could settle into my spell.

I ran in to bowl and it landed exactly where I wanted it to.

BANG! He flat-batted it ferociously back towards me and in my follow-through I was powerless to prevent it striking me flush on the top of my head.

I went down instantly and protectively grabbed hold of my now-pounding head. Aware of being surrounded by concerned players, I heard a familiar voice.

'Fletch, Fletch, talk to me,' it sounded as if Steven Mullaney was in tears.

I tried to take stock of what had happened and decided to lift my head and take my hands away. It was like you see in a horror movie, blood spurting out everywhere, desperate to make its escape.

It shook me, to be honest and I thought, 'I could be in a bit of trouble here.'

The ball had hit me flush on the top of the head and I was expecting further consequences, anticipating that I would black out at any second.

It was a scary second or two before my mindset changed a little. 'Am I going to keel over or am I going to be all right?'

By now James Pipe, the Notts physio, was with me. He just legged it on the field as soon as it happened. Much later, people re-watched it on Sky Sports and they say he was beside me within 11 seconds of it happening.

* * *

James Pipe: 'The first thing I remember is hearing the batsman smash the ball and there was a crack, like a gun going off, as he hit it out of the screws. Then there was another crack as the ball struck Fletch and ricocheted away.

'As he fell forwards and dropped to his knees I grabbed my kit and raced on. I hadn't been certain where the ball had struck him and can remember just hoping that his airways were clear.

'Upon reaching him I could see that wasn't a concern. His scalp had been split and blood was pouring out. Externally, it didn't look good, so I quickly covered his head to screen it from the other players.

'Fletch was surprisingly calm and relaxed and it was a huge relief when he spoke to me. "I know I shouldn't but I feel all right," he said.

'I asked him a few questions and he was able to answer them all coherently.

'Thankfully he was alert and knew where he was and what the score was.

'Then he shocked me by trying to get up. I told him that there was no rush and he should stay down but he persisted, so I went with it and he was able to stand up and walk off with me.

'Back in the medical room the team at Warwickshire were fantastic but I thought it must have started raining when all the other players started coming off the pitch.

'One or two of them were visibly upset and I know it must have freaked a few of them out because we're not accustomed to seeing cricketers with oxygen masks on.'

* * *

Pipey was brilliant with me and there were lots of other medics there once we'd gone back inside the dressing room. The next thing I knew they were putting jabs in my head and stitching the wound.

The accident had happened with quite a new white ball and the new raised seam had more than likely split my skull.

During this procedure I was laid out in the little physio's room at the side of the main dressing room and it had a glass or Perspex partition so you could see through into the other side.

Laid there, I suddenly began to see some of the other Notts players entering the main room, so thought it must have started raining and the umpires had brought them off.

Their reactions suggested something different though. Riki Wessels was crying and Mullaney was crying. I could even see Samit crying, so thought it must be really serious. I thought maybe KFC had shut down!

Then I saw one man who wasn't crying. It was Alex Hales. He'd noticed me through the partition and made eye contact before slowly raising his middle finger in my direction, giving me 'the bird'.

My mate taking the p**s; it made me smile and was just the tonic that I needed right then.

I was obviously aware that I was the centre of attention right then and one or two players got as far as sticking their head around the door to see how I was. With an oxygen mask over my face I couldn't say a deal to them but hopefully a few cheeky 'thumbs up' signals would have settled their concerns.

They then carted me into the back of an ambulance and we headed off to the Queen Elizabeth Hospital in Birmingham.

Pipey stayed with me throughout, as I was whisked from room to room, assessed and given all sorts of head scans and tests.

It appeared as if I'd been pretty lucky. One doctor told me that the impact had occurred on the hardest part of my head but they did insist that I needed to stay in overnight for observation.

Sleep was difficult but I managed to nod off every now and then, only to keep getting awoken every two or three hours so that a nurse could check my blood pressure and temperature and that sort of thing.

One of the nurses looking after me was very nice. We chatted and she told me that she was from Kenya originally.

It became clear that she wasn't aware of what had happened to me because at around three in the morning she told me that they should have weighed me and checked my height when I'd arrived.

Reluctantly, I got out of bed and went to the scales – I think they were wrong because they were showing I'd put on two kilos (!) – and then she did my height.

I stood with my back to the wall and then she slid the headpiece straight down, firmly, on to the wound, making me yelp with pain.

She was so startled she forgot to take the reading and asked me to do it again. Once more, there was very little in the way of tender, loving care as she repeated her actions.

Blood started trickling down the side of my face then and she started apologising, 'Oh I'm sorry, I'm sorry.'

It was no laughing matter really, as she'd opened up the stitches and they needed to be re-done but Pipey couldn't help but chuckle at my predicament:

'I stayed at the hospital with him and was doing my notes while he slept. When the nurse came and split his stitches I nearly choked on my Twix at how it looked but typically Luke was brilliant with her and just took it all in his stride.'

Later that Sunday morning my phone was returned to me. With it being a televised match we'd all had to hand our phones in, regulations that were in force to prevent anyone passing on any lucrative betting information, should they be crazy enough to risk their careers doing so.

At the time I had no idea how big a deal it had become, with hundreds of messages from well-wishers.

Apart from family, friends and supporters there was a nice message from Freddie Flintoff. It was all a little surreal, I felt like a celebrity for a day – a celebrity with a very sore head.

The results of my scans were mixed. I hadn't fractured my skull but it had caused a bleed on the brain and the specialists immediately told me that I couldn't play again that season – something that was tough to hear when there were almost three full months of matches left.

They were concerned about what is called 'second hit syndrome' and the consequences, although unlikely, of being hit in the same place again, so soon. The worry was that my brain would go to mush if that happened – a phrase that caused nothing but sarcasm when I told my unsympathetic teammates.

While I had been the unfortunate one to receive the blow to the head, I also felt for Sam Hain. He certainly hadn't intended me any harm when he played that shot and, although it had just been an unlucky accident, I was delighted to hear from him.

* * *

Sam Hain: 'It was his first delivery and I skipped down the pitch to him and just middled it. I saw it strike him on the head and there were people around him quickly.

'I backed away to square leg and tried to take in what had happened. There was a long delay and I remember not wanting the game to continue but they decided that it should.

'I went out to bat again and was out almost immediately. The rest of the evening almost seemed to pass me by in slow-motion.

'The next day I wrote out and deleted between five and ten texts as I tried to find the right words, before eventually just sent him a message saying, "Mate, I hope you're ok."'

18

Sick Of Jeremy Kyle

OVER THE next couple of months I was urged to do nothing but rest, so got into a lazy routine of watching *The Jeremy Kyle Show* each morning.

My excuse was that I was looking to see if any of my old schoolmates were on!

For a while I became a focus of attention for the media who, while concerned, kept ringing up wanting to do a piece with me. I said to one that I'd now got into a fairly steady routine of doing nothing and saw a headline of, 'FLETCHER SICK OF JEREMY KYLE'.

Sorry Jezza, nothing personal!

With several weeks of the cricket season still left to play I couldn't stay away from the lads for long and kept up with their fortunes by doing some local radio commentaries.

For the second time in a few weeks I was reminded of Alex Hales's talent as I watched him blitz a brilliant double hundred at Derby.

During that championship match I received a query from Sky Sports, wondering if I'd be interested in doing some stuff for them. It necessitated a day of on-the-job training with the brilliant David Fulton.

Fults is now a fantastic broadcaster and event host, having spent a successful playing career with Kent. On top of all that, he's also another Forest fan!

Brother Sam drove me all the way down to the Ageas Bowl, where Fults was covering a game and he gave me a very thorough insight into life as a television reporter.

Having passed my induction I was given a match – Notts Outlaws v Birmingham Bears at Trent Bridge.

It was the return match between the two, just a few weeks after I'd been hit. They wanted me to do the odd piece to camera and get one or two interviews for them, and in particular they wanted me to talk it all through again with Sam Hain.

* * *

Sam Hain: 'It had taken me a while to get over what had happened and I'd tried to shut it out and move on. But when we played them in the return a few weeks later Sky Sports thought it would be a good idea to reunite us and for Fletch to interview me.

'All I could say was, "Mate, you cost me four runs."'

Everyone was so pleased that Fletch came through it okay and we've been able to carry on playing against each other ever since. He's an outstanding bowler, who enjoys getting in a battle and wears his heart on his sleeve.'

* * *

As with most neurological cases I had to surrender my driving licence after the injury and was told not to drive for six months or to do any physical activity for the first three months. The club remedied that by getting me a bicycle, so I had to pedal the three miles or so to Trent Bridge once I was able to.

It was awful biking in through the winter, the dark nights and early mornings, slipping on black ice and dodging erratic drivers. Always seemingly cycling up an incline with the wind in my face.

One of the worst things about the injury was that it had happened in a televised game and had been seen by absolutely everybody. It meant that everyone had to be seen to do the correct thing with regards to my recovery.

Nick Pearce, the ECB doctor, came round to take my stitches out and paid me one or two more visits to check how I was getting on.

There were discussions within the game about head protection being provided for bowlers in the future but nothing came of it.

One or two suggested I might have to carry on looking like Petr Cech, the former Chelsea and Arsenal goalkeeper, who wore a protective helmet after suffering a fractured skull but that's as far as it went and I didn't push it.

Certainly, I'd have been happy to wear one if the medics had instructed me to do so and it had been the only way of continuing my career but I got the feeling that the technology wasn't there and companies would have been wary in case it failed.

The odds are that someone will be hit again while playing cricket. I just hope they are as fortunate as I was.

One of the lighter moments in my recovery came when I was given an IQ test, something we do annually normally.

At the start of the year I'd done mine on the flight out to pre-season training in Barbados. I'd had a few beers at Manchester Airport the evening before and was feeling a bit ropey. I scored 85 per cent.

Having been hit on the head, they gave it to me again. I scored 100 per cent this time!

* * *

Notts made it through to T20 Finals Day in 2017, the sixth occasion they'd reached that stage of a tournament they were yet to win.

Edgbaston was packed solid, with Hampshire, Glamorgan and the Birmingham Bears making up the quartet of qualifiers.

Although my season was over I was delighted to be able to join the Notts squad for the day and spent it doing a fair amount of media work and some radio commentary.

Birmingham made the most of their home advantage to see off Glamorgan in the opening semi-final and then the Outlaws had the better of Hampshire in the second.

Finals Day has become one of the major highlights of the domestic season and the atmosphere was unbelievable once again.

David 'Bumble' Lloyd and Freddie Flintoff, both working for Sky Sports, whipped the crowd into a frenzy beforehand.

Bumble was dressed in black and did his best Johnny Cash impersonation before Freddie arrived on the scene to give a rendition of Elvis Presley's 'Suspicious Minds', dressed in an all-white jumpsuit.

The pair then united in front of the Hollies Stand to get the place rocking with a chorus or two of 'Sweet Caroline'.

Then it was back to the cricket and with me watching on from the Edgbaston radio boxes Samit and BT put on 132 for us, setting it up for Dan Christian to plunder 24 from the final over.

Birmingham's pursuit of a victory target of 191 failed to gather any sort of momentum and the writing was on the wall for them long before Harry Gurney completed his spell of 4-17.

For the first time Notts Outlaws were domestic T20 champions and had secured their second trophy of the summer.

At around this point someone from the Edgbaston club came and asked if I'd like to be involved in the presentation ceremony. I thought it was a nice touch from them.

This, if you like, would take things full circle. My injury had occurred at Edgbaston in this same competition, and now I was back there a few weeks later to see Notts win the trophy.

I made my way pitchside, having been asked to be involved but no one acknowledged my presence, leaving me feeling like a bit of a spare part. 'I'm here!'

Perhaps if I had helped out, then things might have gone a little smoother. Getting showered in champagne has become something of an occupational hazard but is always enjoyable when you're celebrating a win.

Not everyone feels the same though.

The NatWest T20 Blast trophy is a big piece of metal with sharp corners and the lady from the sponsors, that had come to present it, had bought a new frock and had her hair done for the occasion.

Weighing up the situation quickly she had noticed that each of our players had been given a bottle of champagne and were about to spray them.

Rather than presenting the trophy, she thrust it hurriedly towards Dan and made a very hasty exit from the stage to try and avoid the spray.

Unfortunately for the Outlaws captain she'd caught him flush on the left eyelid with the pointy bit of the trophy.

Saluting the fans, Dan's finest moment for the club had him drenched in champagne and with a trickle of red running down his cheek.

In very different ways we'd both spilt blood for the cause.

19

Derby Days

THERE COMES a time when you feel you really belong in county cricket and that's when you've played against every other team and visited all of the major grounds.

Over the first decade of my career I have had many ups and downs travelling around the county circuit.

New grounds and old, each and every week brings a new experience and over the next few pages I'll try and run through a few of my favourite stories from battles against the other 17 counties.

Before then, a word on my favourite playing venue.

There's something very magical about Trent Bridge. I felt a tingle the first time I played there and that's remained with me throughout my career.

It's a wonderful ground just to walk upon, having the feel of a springy freshly-laid carpet and the outfield is lightning fast and unforgiving for a bowler. I call it 'the hoover' because it seems to suck the ball away from the middle and quickly out to the ropes. Walking out to the middle is an experience in itself and one I'll never take for granted. The journey begins as we leave our dressing room at the top of the historic pavilion.

Then the descent begins. Each movement echoing noisily as our studs reverberate on the wooden steps.

Past the opposition dressing room we go – sometimes stalling to have a look in if their door has been left open – and then paying homage to the stars of the past who adorn the pavilion walls.

There's framed photographs of Clive Rice and Tim Robinson lifting trophies, of Richard Hadlee and Derek Randall in their pomp, all Nottinghamshire greats.

As you reach the bottom you begin the walk out under the row of flags, huge billowing pennants that commemorate each of the county's championship wins.

Then the sunlight and the noise hit you as you leave the pavilion and start to take in the view. I enjoy this the most when I'm going out to bat because you're making the journey on your own – soaking it all in, aware that everyone's eyes are upon you.

I always glance to the far end, the Radcliffe Road End, and love to see how many people are up there watching on, with the best view in the house.

When the very top tier is open at that end, for the big one-day or T20 matches, we know it's going to be a huge crowd and the atmosphere will be extra-special.

One of the strangest times to be playing at Trent Bridge is when it coincides with Nottingham Forest also being at home, across the road at the City Ground.

If we're fielding, then Broady, Samit and myself – the Forest fans in our team – like to be at the Radcliffe Road End, in order to clearly hear the roars, the oohs and aahs, and the cheers coming from the football and try to imagine what's going on.

Once the Forest match finishes many of the supporters will come back to the cricket and from the boundary edge tell us what went on.

I've never taken for granted how fortunate I am to play for Notts and am so grateful to the supporters for the way they've got behind me over the years.

There's nothing more than a good local derby to really get them going and, as I've discovered, fixtures against our near neighbours usually throw up a talking point or two.

The rivalry between Nottinghamshire and Derbyshire has always been pretty intense, although thankfully not quite as vociferous as some meetings between the football teams from each city.

Nevertheless, some Friday evening T20 Blast matches between us have got rather rowdy and it's not unusual for players from both sides to get a fair amount of personal abuse.

As a Nottingham Forest fan I've had to deal with quite a bit of mickey-taking from Derby County supporters but always enjoy a little bit of friendly banter with them.

Occasionally it gets a bit daft though and sometimes they step over the line, usually when there's drink involved.

As a club we always look forward to our trips to Derby and know that we'll be in for a spiky reception.

Thankfully, most of the time – but not always – we've had the upper hand in fixtures against our nearest and dearest during my playing career.

My first T20 appearances for Notts came during the 2009 season and my third match was away at Derby. They were rattling along and on course for a good score. Wavell Hinds and Greg Smith had put on over 100 together but then it all kicked off.

Hinds, a big, left-handed West Indian, hoisted Graeme Swann towards long-off where Darren Pattinson took a catch right on the fence.

Patto, who had made one Test appearance for England a year earlier but had spent much of his life in Australia, claimed that it was clean, despite a crescendo of noise advising him and the umpires that the rope had been touched as he completed the dismissal.

Hinds was given out and the volley of abuse that followed was something to behold. Patto is no shrinking violet and I'm sure most of the big mouths wouldn't have dared to front up to him in a one-to-one situation.

I managed to pick up a couple of wickets and we were left to chase their score of 158/5. It was immediately apparent that earlier events weren't going to be quickly forgotten. John

Morris, a former England Test cricketer who perhaps became best known for co-piloting a Tiger Moth alongside David Gower, was Derbyshire's head coach.

From his position on the pavilion balcony he spewed forth his opinions for the rest of the evening and it's fair to say it all became a bit feisty.

Sat in the dug-out, taking it all in, I wondered if this was how it always was.

Meanwhile, Morris's mood wasn't improved by our decision to send out Swanny at the top of the order. Fired up, he produced something he'd never done before – and didn't come close to repeating again – as he blazed his way to an unbeaten 90 off just 47 balls to see us to victory with five overs to spare. Fun times.

* * *

We've all got those 'glad I was there' moments and right at the top of my list is the day that Samit Patel went viral on the internet.

In 2013 Derbyshire returned to Division One of the County Championship for the first time in many years and we went there in the early weeks of the season for an eagerly anticipated clash.

Either side of tea on the second day James Taylor and Samit put together a decent stand. Taylor went on to make a hundred and we eventually won the match on the final day but the lasting memory came with the first-innings dismissal of Samit.

He pushed the ball into the covers and noticed a slight fumble by the fielder, Billy Godleman. Samit set off, for what would have been a sharp single.

Titch (James Taylor) yelled 'no' immediately. There had been a bit of moisture around all day and the outfield had been a bit slippery but there was no way of anticipating what happened next. Samit responded to the call by trying to stop his forward momentum but as he put the brakes on his legs were whipped from underneath him and he went down, straight on to his backside, with an almighty bump.

Laying prostrate on the ground, he was powerless to do anything as Godleman recovered the ball and returned it to the wicketkeeper for the easiest run-out ever executed.

Around 100 yards away the rest of the team were watching from the sanctuary of the away dressing room. I was sat with Baz, Broady, Ed Cowan and one or two more when the wicket went down and none of us could believe our eyes.

We knew that Samit would be raging though and didn't want to get caught in the crossfire.

There was a race to get into the back room out of the way. I headed for a single cubicle but kept the door slightly open so that I could see what was going off.

From my vantage point I could see Baz and Broady and witnessed how hard they were trying to stifle their laughter.

Samit made his way back into the dressing room. Mick Newell was clearly disgusted and was eyeing him with his arms folded.

Everything was quiet, although there was a lot of silent tittering going on. Then Mick started laughing and everyone else joined in. The whole place erupted, with Broady one of the most vocal.

* * *

Stuart Broad: 'When someone gets out it's natural to stay out of their way, you don't want to make eye contact with them, so when Samit got out I thought it best to go and put my thigh pad on ready for when I would be batting.

'Samit came back into the dressing room and was acting all angrily, saying that "it's a disgrace, Titch has run me out" and all that.

'From where I was I could see Fletcher's cheeky face giggling, but he had it under control. I struggled to keep my composure and stared at the floor trying not to laugh but there was more and more giggling from Fletch and from Hales and they were struggling to keep it in.

'Then Mick Newell set us all off by saying to Samit, "Hard luck. Where there's blame there's a claim!"'

* * *

Poor Samit. He got teased terribly and his pain continues to this day. It's sometimes amazing what attracts online attention and that run-out proves the point. I think it's had something like two million hits on YouTube, although one million were by me!

* * *

Did I mention that I was a Forest fan? Growing up and supporting the club my big hero was Stuart Pearce, so imagine my delight when 'Psycho' returned to the City Ground as manager in the summer of 2014.

He'd only been in the job for a week or two when we were drawn to play Derbyshire at home in the quarter-finals of the Royal London One-Day Cup.

Prior to the match we were instructed to arrive at Trent Bridge slightly earlier than normal and to meet in the players' dining room at the top of the pavilion.

Typically, for whatever reason, something or other held me up slightly and I was a minute or two late in arriving. I turned the door handle to go in and was immediately halted in my tracks.

Stuart Pearce was sat there, having been invited to give us a pre-match pep talk by Mick Newell. I was in awe of the man, not only a great footballer but also an inspirational speaker.

It was riveting to hear how he built himself up for local derbies and hear all about his proudest moments for club and country.

We all learnt a lot that day and went out and produced a stunning performance to hammer our near-neighbours.

* * *

You never know with professional sport what might be just around the corner. Take our Royal London match at Derby in 2019 for example. After winning the toss and batting, the home side were 153/0 after 30 overs. Billy Godleman, he of the Samit run-out fame, and Luis Reece were going like trains.

My first seven overs had brought scant reward and figures of 0-50. When I returned to the attack for the closing hurrah all smart money was on me getting a good hiding. Godleman had passed his century and the middle order were champing at the bit to get stuck in.

In my eighth over I clean-bowled Leus du Plooy, in my ninth I had Godleman caught behind and then I yorked three others within the space of five balls to finish with 5-56, my best one-day figures – not a bad turn-around!

* * *

For a Notts lad, loud and proud, you may have noticed that I've not really had a go at the 'enemy' and that's because I briefly jumped ship and played four matches for Derbyshire on loan at the start of 2016.

My debut for them was away against Gloucestershire at Bristol and while it may have been a new dressing room for me, there was one very familiar face.

Andy Carter, who had started at Notts at the same time as me, had moved along the A52 that winter and was also playing his first match for his new county.

We opened the bowling together, which was another nice touch, but the surface didn't really suit either of us as the match petered out into a high-scoring draw, with hundreds from Derbyshire's Wayne Madsen and Chesney Hughes and Gloucestershire's Chris Dent and Liam Norwell.

That match started a trend that continued throughout my stay with Derbyshire, with all four being drawn.

I didn't get too many wickets for them but got lots of overs under my belt, which stood me in good stead for when I returned to Nottingham.

20

Cold, North-East Tears

THERE'S USUALLY a mixed feeling among our group whenever we set off to play against Durham in the north-east.

On the one hand, we know it'll be bloody freezing, no matter what time of year. There was one occasion when we actually played up there in snow, with most players having to wear bobble hats to keep out the cold.

On the other hand though, we know that if we're lucky we may get the opportunity for a good night out in their Loveshack nightclub!

As I'm sure you will have gathered by now, I generally try and play cricket with a laugh and a joke if I can but I'll never be able to forget the time I was reduced to tears in a County Championship match against Durham.

Hopefully, I will get to score a hundred in first-class cricket before I retire but if I don't I only have myself to blame, as I should have reached the magic number up at Chester-le-Street in 2017.

Sent in as nightwatchman, just before the close, I managed to do my job and made it through to stumps at the end of the first day unscathed.

For whatever reason I felt good about myself at breakfast the following morning and told whoever would listen that this was the day I was going to score a hundred, a fairly bold pronouncement for someone who only had three runs to his name and had been heard to spout such nonsense many times before.

I resumed my innings cautiously but avoided any calamities in surviving the entire morning session, reaching my fifty just before lunch, which we took with seven wickets down.

James Pattinson had joined me out in the middle and we had little trouble in negotiating the opening hour of the second session.

Nothing was happening for the Durham seam attack of Graham Onions, Chris Rushworth, Mark Wood and Paul Coughlin and it was clear that they were hankering for a new ball to aid their chances.

On came Ryan Pringle, the off-spinner, mainly just to soak up a few overs and give the quicks a brief rest. His gentle turn and deep-set field offered little threat as I was nicely set. I picked him off for three boundaries and a two in the 76th over to move my score along from 78 to 92.

Paul Collingwood, the home captain, then decided to have a go and handed his cap to the umpire for the first time in the match.

A former England World T20 winner, Colly rarely bowled by that stage of his career but had enjoyed a reputation as a 'golden arm' for many years.

There were just four overs remaining until Durham could ask for a new ball and I could smell an opportunity to get some free and easy runs.

Collingwood's first delivery was chopped fiercely away by Patto. How many could we run or would it reach the fence?

I set off like a hare out of the trap until disaster struck.

Keaton Jennings, in the gully, had dived to make a sensational stop..

With it being early in the season, the grass was really lush. I tried to slam the anchors on but lost my footing and went straight down on my backside, losing my bat in the process.

Almost in slow-motion I knew I had little time to recover my ground but scrambled to my feet and threw myself towards the sanctuary of my crease.

Crazily, I even attempted to dive and run my bat in, even though I'd dropped it. Jennings didn't offer me a reprieve. His return to Collingwood was delivered with pinpoint accuracy and I was run out by a country mile for 92.

It was stupid. I still think there probably should have been an easy single there as I'd managed to get halfway down the track and almost back – but it wasn't to be.

This was one of the first times that I'd been close to crying on a cricket pitch. I'd done all of the hard work and got so close but had again thrown away the opportunity of that maiden ton.

It had been there for the taking and everyone knew it. I should probably admit that the sympathetic round of applause I received as I trudged off was probably acknowledged with a tear or two in my eye.

So my wait for a first-class hundred goes on but I have hit one for Nottinghamshire's seconds. It came against Derbyshire at Lady Bay in 2010 and I scored 106.

The only other times I've reached three figures have been in club cricket and in a warm-up match in Potchefstroom, when the Notts squad was split in half. Still counts, yes?

* * *

I've always had a pretty torrid time against Durham. Graham Onions has hit me on the head a few times and so did his former teammate Mitch Claydon.

One match up there he did me with a lively bumper and hit me flush on the badge. Being 'sconed', we call it in the game.

Fair play to Mitch, he came up and asked if I was okay.

We'd often shared a laugh or two in the past and I responded with, 'If you ever do that to me again I'll pick this stump up and stab you with it.'

I tried to keep a straight face and look serious but he just laughed back at me.

He pitched the next one up and I got off strike.

Mitch was bowling quickly and I thought I don't fancy much more of that. I was batting with Mull and told him that I'd stay down the other end where Ian Blackwell was bowling his left-arm spinners. I thought I'd be more comfortable down there and told him so.

You can probably guess the rest.

First ball from Blackwell I pushed straight into the hands of silly point, straight off the face of the bat.

Mull always reminds me of that one, the day I felt confident enough to take on Ian Blackwell!

* * *

One other Durham memory that springs to mind was playing against them on my T20 debut at Trent Bridge in 2009.

Having already represented Notts in first-class and one-day cricket it was nice to complete the set with my first appearance in the shortest format.

Although full of nerves, I got off to the perfect start, dismissing Phil Mustard in the first over of the match as the punchy left-hander picked out Baz for me at deep cover.

I also dismissed former Notts player Will Smith, to claim 2-23 from my four overs. My T20 career was up and running.

21

Superman

ONE OF my first away trips with Nottinghamshire's second team was to play against Essex at a place called Wickford. We won the match and I did okay but the thing I remember most was before the match had started. I suddenly realised in the changing room that I was sat next to Stephen Fleming.

The New Zealand international, who was skippering Notts that year, was just returning to the game after injury and had fancied getting his timing back in sync with a knock for the seconds.

It's not often that I feel any sympathy for the opposition but on this particular day the Essex bowler Jahid Ahmed looked to have Fleming plumb lbw first ball. He appeared to be stone dead but the umpire bottled it and didn't give him out.

The Kiwi legend got into his stride and knocked off a stylish hundred in no time before tucking his bat under his arm and clearing off. Job done. I don't recall if I actually spoke to Fleming that day or not but it was a long, long time before our paths crossed again. Towards the back end of 2019 I received a pleasant surprise when I was sat at home watching the live televised draft for cricket's inaugural The Hundred competition.

Fleming had been chosen as the head coach of the Trent Bridge-based side, Trent Rockets. Perhaps with the help of a kindly word or two from the Notts contingent who were helping him with the picks, to my astonishment he selected me in the sixth or seventh round.

My one-time changing room companion was to become my new gaffer.

* * *

We've had one or two good hidings against Essex at Chelmsford during my career. I remember Maurice Chambers running through us in both innings during our 2010 County Championship match there.

More recently, I did enjoy some personal success there. Although it eventually turned into another heavy defeat I did claim some personal success by taking five wickets in their first innings in 2019.

Other than that, my favourite visit to Chelmsford involved being on the balcony for the One-Day Cup semi-final in 2017. The home crowd were hushed as Samit Patel and Steven Mullaney each scored hundreds as we completed a record run-chase to reach the final.

Essex had scored 370/5 and their supporters were already celebrating loud and proud before Samit shared in a stand of

100 with Brendan Taylor and then 185 with Mull to get us over the line.

* * *

Dan Lawrence was unlucky. So unlucky.

The Essex batsman must have thought he'd got off the mark in true style when he timed his second delivery so sweetly in a County Championship match against us at Trent Bridge.

Fresh to the crease, he clipped the ball in the air towards the fence at deep mid-on. Yours truly, some 30 yards from the bat, didn't fancy the long chase in vain towards the pavilion fence so I leapt as high as I could.

Miraculously, the ball stuck in my outstretched hand. I can only imagine Dan's reaction as I plunged back to earth clutching my shiny red prize.

Lyndon James, the bowler, was making his Nottinghamshire debut, so he was jubilant as he rushed towards me.

If you weren't there and want to visualise me flying through the air like Superman, please indulge yourself.

Testimony to how good it was came from one Twitter poll I saw later. In a far from successful season for us, that was voted as the outstanding moment.

Unlucky Dan!

Bowling during my short loan spell down the A52 with Derbyshire

Sharing a joke with umpire Nick Cook after picking up a wicket for Surrey

I enjoyed my time in New Zealand with Wellington but on this occasion the shirt was more impressive than the shot

Royal London One-Day Cup Final at Lord's 2017, bowling Gareth Batty and a special salute for family and friends

Enjoying our win with Samit and Peter Moores

With Baz and Patto

With Kirsty (left) and the great BT (right)

BIR 30-0
3
20
TARGET 159
HAIN 16*
BELL 11
FLETCHER

sky SPORTS 2 HD
LIVE

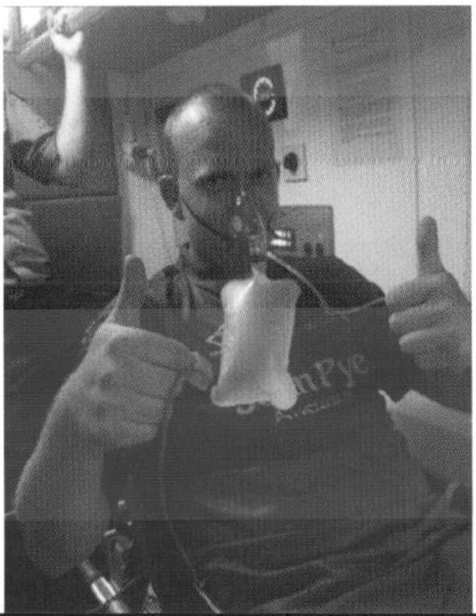

In the absence of a rubber duck, Steven Mullaney has his uses!

Proud as Punch! Receiving my county cap from Chris Read, alongside Riki Wessels (left) and Harry Gurney (right)

Starting young, Freddie helping the groundstaff out at Trent Bridge

Sometimes things just go your way. Yorking Birmingham Bears' Laurie Evans at Trent Bridge

Having fun with my old mate Marcus Trescothick

The infamous mid-pitch collision with Stuart Broad. Only 'pretty boy' received any attention from the medics!

Quietly celebrating hitting the winning run v Lancashire

Loved my time at Hooters

Far Left: The best beer is always a winning beer. Sharing a success with Jake Ball, Harry Gurney and Stuart Broad

Right: A night out with Kirsty, to see Freddie Flintoff in Fat Friends

Things change quickly. We only got as far as the press photo shoot ahead of The Hundred in 2020

What it's all about – Kirsty, Freddie and I welcoming Rosie into the family

22

Never Seen Anything Like It

IT DOES sting a bit when you dominate a County Championship match but then can't get over the line and complete the victory.

One such occasion saw us force our opponents to follow on, quickly had them five down in their second innings and still didn't win.

At Cardiff in 2017 we had Glamorgan on toast for the first three days and turned up to complete the formalities on the final day.

We'd started our Division Two campaign with a trio of convincing victories that season and aimed to leave South Wales with a fourth straight win.

Things couldn't have gone much better, until we ran into Colin Ingram and Chris Cooke.

At 11 o'clock on the fourth morning they resumed the Glamorgan second innings on 212/5, still a long way away from making us bat again.

We threw everything at them but they resisted until lunch, no mean achievement given the circumstances.

The afternoon session saw Glamorgan nudge past us and move ahead overall but we weren't concerned as there was still plenty of time to complete the win once we'd broken this partnership.

Only we didn't break the partnership.

Not by tea.

And not before five o'clock when we all shook hands on a draw.

For the first – and hopefully only – time in my career I had been in the field all day and we didn't take a wicket.

Ingram finished on 155 not out and Cooke remained undefeated on 113. They'd added an unbroken 226 together and frustrated us for the entire final day.

Chris Read had gone off with an injured hand, leaving Riki Wessels to take the wicketkeeper's gloves. Otherwise everyone else had a bowl that day, including Cheteshwar Pujara, the Indian Test star who was making his Nottinghamshire debut.

'I've never seen anything like it,' he said afterwards. He wasn't the only one.

* * *

Perhaps the most testing conditions I've ever had to bat in came in a match against Glamorgan. I spent the opening month of the 2016 season on loan at Derbyshire and we faced the Welsh side in a County Championship match at Derby.

A few flakes of snow had just started to fall when I made my way out to the middle. It progressively got harder and harder until I found myself facing Michael Hogan in a near-blizzard.

The snow was coming at right angles straight into my face and I could hardly see a thing, yet the umpires let play continue like this for a few deliveries before common sense kicked in!

23

Second Time Lucky

ONE OF my first big disappointments as a Notts player came against Gloucestershire. Everyone dreams of doing well in sport, of winning trophies and reaching finals.

The first time I played in a knockout match came in my second season as a pro. We'd confidently marched through the group phase of the One-Day Cup and had to go down to Bristol for the quarter-final. Ryan Sidebottom had been released from an England squad to join us, meaning we were at full strength and hopeful of doing well.

We opted to bat first but were quickly in trouble at 9/3 and then 40/5 as Steve Kirby and Jon Lewis ran through us.

It was a very early finish as Craig Stearman led them to a one-sided victory. At least we were home early.

* * *

Sometimes you get them, sometimes you don't. At Bristol a few years ago I opened the bowling and thought I'd got

Gloucestershire's Australian Test batsman Cameron Bancroft second ball.

It looked an absolute stonewaller to me. It hit his pads and I thought I was knocking over all three stumps. Unbelievably it was turned down.

In the second innings, in a case of déjà vu, I did him again with the second delivery but I didn't think it wasn't as close as before. This time the finger went up. It's a strange game!

24

Shrek?

AS YOU'LL have already discovered, my first impression of matches against Hampshire involved Dominic Cork trying to knock my head off.

That trend has continued ever since. Whenever we have played against the south coast county they have generally tried to rough me up, with two of their Barbadian stars leading the way.

One year at the Ageas Bowl we were struggling badly against the pace of Tino Best. He'd struck Readie and broken a bone in his hand and had also pinned Lumby. I was really looking forward to going out to bat against him!

The first one he sent down to me was a yorker and I just about managed to dig it out. Any sense of achievement was immediately lost because Tino was in my face scowling.

'Give me your wicket big guy, give me your wicket or I'm gonna hit you in the head, Shrek.'

Shrek?

I knew he wasn't confusing me with former Notts player Charlie Shreck, he actually thought I looked like Shrek – the jolly green giant with the big ears!

'Oh no,' I thought. I managed to survive until the end of the over and went down to have a chat with Samit.

Not for the first time, nor the last, my conversation with our brilliant all-rounder didn't go as I'd expected.

'All right?' he offered.

'Yes mate, you?'

'Listen,' he said. 'It's turning square at this end and Mason Crane is spinning it miles, so I'd better take him.'

So what he was really implying was that I should be the sacrificial lamb to face Tino's 95mph rockets, while he 'bravely' attempted to negotiate the spinner.

Karma is a wonderful thing, because Samit then got out to Crane, leaving me in self-preservation mode at the other end.

I didn't know whether to laugh or cry but didn't really have much time to focus on anything but the job in hand.

To be fair to Tino he didn't try and bump me once. Everything was pitched up but he was far too quick for me. In fact, that burst was about the fastest I'd ever faced.

I was scared stiff and honestly thought he was going to kill me.

If it wasn't Tino trying to get me down there, it was his Barbados teammate Fidel Edwards. The word on the circuit was that Fidel was on a cash-per-wicket bonus when he joined Hampshire, so understandably he always wanted to come back on and polish off the tail – free and easy wickets to boost his bank balance.

Whenever I've played against him it has always been my ill fortune to bat just as soon as he's taken a second new ball.

With his slingy, almost round-arm action, he's got a very different style than most other quick bowlers and I find him very difficult to pick up.

I'm sure he's very grateful that I've never delayed him out there for too long!

Fidel was one of the Hampshire players we faced when we set off for a very unusual away trip in 2019.

For the first time in 57 years they were staging a home match on the Isle of Wight. Notts had previously played a championship match on the island, way back in 1957 but this was a new thing for us all.

Travelling to a game by ferry was not something I'd ever anticipated doing but we all boarded at Southampton and set off.

To be honest, there was plenty of nautical jollities around and it seemed more like we were going on our holidays than to a professional sporting contest. At best, it felt as if we may have been going to a benefit game.

All that changed, of course, once we'd got there and the facilities at the Newclose ground were magnificent. A very good crowd, backed up by plenty of Notts fans that had travelled down, came out to support the teams. Like so many matches that summer we missed an opportunity to press home an advantage and were hurried to defeat after second innings centuries from Sam Northeast and Ajinkya Rahane had put the hosts on top.

It was a match we should have done much better in and as we made our way back across the Solent there was a feeling that one way or another we'd missed the boat.

25

Fragments

I WAS still a young lad when I went to Canterbury for the first time with Notts and knew I'd been taken along to do all the menial tasks associated with being 12th man.

It was freezing cold as well, a little more than about four degrees out, causing most of the players to wear their beanie hats.

The Notts players made life difficult for me and had me rushing in and out all day on errands for them. On one particular occasion though, I brought things to a very sudden and dramatic halt.

The sliding doors to the changing rooms looked as if they had taken a bit of a battering over the years but they were no match for yours truly.

I was too rough for them as I slid the doors open for the thousandth time that day. They spectacularly came off at the hinges and tipped up, smashing into a million fragments of glass.

It went everywhere, all over the dressing room and into players' kit bags, shoes, everything. I recall Chris Read being particularly disgruntled because a lot of it went inside his helmet.

I was mortified, it was hardly the way for a youngster to create the right impression. The noise had been so dramatic that it had caused play to stop and everyone was looking at me. I've never been so embarrassed and could feel myself turning beetroot red.

* * *

As with most county dressing rooms, a good deal of time is spent analysing the opposition and their strengths and weaknesses.

Before our 2010 home match with Kent it was drummed into me about where to bowl to Martin van Jaarsveld, the South African international who was in prime form around that stage of his career.

He had quite a high backlift and it was heavily underlined on our chalk board that we must bowl full and straight to him.

We made Kent follow on and early in their second innings I got one to nip back beautifully to bowl Rob Key.

Out came van Jaarsveld and I was saying to myself as I ran in, 'Full and straight, full and straight.'

I put the ball exactly where I wanted it, his bat came down too late and only his pad prevented the ball from crashing into middle and off. Plumb lbw, one of the most satisfying deliveries I've ever sent down.

26

Don't Wanna Play No More

I MADE my County Championship debut as part of a five-man bowling attack in a drawn match at Old Trafford against Lancashire in 2009. Ryan Sidebottom, Paul Franks, Andre Adams and Graeme Swann had all got themselves among the wickets and I knew that all eyes were on the debutant as I came back for a third spell with them seven down.

Thank heavens for Ali Brown.

* * *

Ali Brown: 'I was glad to play a part in his first championship wicket. Kyle Hogg, a left-hander, was on strike and I was fielding at third slip.

'Fletch bowled a great length and got good bounce, so it gave me a little bit more time to react than when people like Sidebottom were bowling and I took it down towards second slip's knee somewhere.

'No sooner had I pouched the catch than Fletch was all over me, nearly squeezing me to death in his delight.'

* * *

There was also a bit of a fuss made when I scored my first run, later on in the match. Oliver Newby was the bowler and after I'd scored my first run I heard Graeme Swann bellow loudly from the balcony, 'First of many!'

That was the good side of Swanny. One of my earliest T20 matches was also at Old Trafford and I made the mistake of mis-fielding off his bowling.

At least it gave Chris Read a good laugh, 'Fletch was out in the deep and they ran a two to him, instead of it being just a single. Swanny really bawled him out for it, gave him a properly hard time.

'Fletch genuinely looked like he wanted to pack it all in there and then. He said to me, "I don't wanna play any more if he's going to be like that!"'

27

The Follow-Through

JAKE BALL'S home debut for Notts came in a one-day match against Leicestershire. You may have heard the term follow-through in cricket. This was a day that still embarrasses me when I think about it.

I opened the bowling and didn't feel very well. I'd got stomach-ache and had cramps and felt a bit bloaty. You know what it's like, right? You feel that it's perhaps a bit of trapped wind, 'better out than in' and all that.

I was at mid-off chatting to Bally as he was about to bowl his first over and I knew I couldn't stand it any longer. My intention was to have a crafty fart and clear the blockage.

Things didn't go to plan. Instead of relief, I was experiencing a very different sensation and was very concerned, as cricket flannels can be rather revealing.

I turned to Bally and asked if he would carry out a preliminary inspection to check and see if there were signs of any damage.

Jake still laughs about it today, 'Readie [Chris Read] chucked me the ball but as I started to run in I heard Fletch shouting, "Stop, stop. I think I've s**t myself!"

'Unfortunately, as I happened to be closest to him he asked me to verify his worst fears. He turned round and lowered his kegs to reveal white cycling shorts underneath and the tell-tale damage.

'He was in a right state and told the umpires he'd have to go off. Then he started to make apologies to everyone as he ran off.

'It made me laugh so much I completely forgot about being nervous and what I was doing.'

If there is any pride to be salvaged from this unfortunate episode it comes from how well Jake bowled. He picked up a couple of Leicestershire wickets straight away and showed everyone what a talent he is.

I'm claiming an assist for his wickets, as my little 'accident' had made him laugh so much and settled him down – even if it had the opposite effect on my stomach!

28

Down By The Toilets

I'M SURE every county cricketer in the country would back me up and say the same thing. 'Uxbridge is all right but…'

If you happen to find yourself in the same division as Middlesex then you want to play them at Lord's.

It's all right for those county sides in the south as they may get several opportunities to play there each season, with the white-ball competitions being regionalised.

For the rest of us, it's not so often.

Apart from all the tradition, the Home of Cricket is just a tremendous place to spend four days, although it did take me some time to work out the slope.

I'd heard that if you lay down on the ground on the tavern side you couldn't see the front few rows of the Grandstand, so I had to try that out for myself when I went there for the first time.

That was for a match in which I happened to be 12th man, ideal for a first-timer, giving me plenty of opportunity to have a good nose around.

It didn't stop me getting into a spot of trouble though.

With a drinks break coming up I managed to get everybody's order ready in time and went bombing down the stairs. Down one flight, down two flights and then down again, expecting to emerge into the Long Room.

I found myself in front of the toilets.

I'd gone too far down and was in a right flap. It took me quite a few moments to get my bearings and I got a good ticking off when I eventually made it out on to the field.

As I'm sure you will have heard, the catering is always exceptional at Lord's and for someone who loves his grub I couldn't believe it the first time. Fridges full of a variety of soft drinks, a dressing room attendant who will go and get bacon cobs if you asked him and sensational three-course lunches.

* * *

It's always nice to hit the pegs, no matter what level you are playing at. One year I took a hat-trick for Notts seconds in the semi-final of the one-day competition.

We were playing Middlesex at Radlett and I clean bowled Ryan Higgins, Tom Helm and Ryan Patel with consecutive deliveries to secure our place in the final.

29

Simple Game

MY FIRST proper appearance at Trent Bridge was on my debut for the county, a one-day match in the Friends Provident Trophy in 2008.

We were playing against Northamptonshire and both Adam Voges and Darren Pattinson were also playing their first match for the county.

Voges, the experienced Australian international, had joined as our overseas player for the start of the season and Pattinson, who had an English passport, had joined us from Victoria.

Mum and Dad were on holiday in Turkey, so missed the occasion. We had already picked up four early wickets when I was brought on to bowl, with South African Nicky Boje on strike.

He couldn't reach the first ball I sent down, a big wide outside off stump. Next up, I got a little closer to him and he played and missed. Third time lucky I got even tighter and he obligingly edged it through to Chris Read.

'It's a simple game,' I thought briefly, before Graeme Swann came flying in, to rugby tackle me to the ground.

* * *

In 2016 I played in possibly the craziest professional one-day match ever to be staged in this country as Notts and Northants rattled up 870 runs in just 98.2 overs.

The record books will simply state that Notts Outlaws defeated Northamptonshire Steelbacks by 20 runs in the North Group of the Royal London One-Day Cup but closer scrutiny will reveal what an extraordinary day it was.

Steve Birks, the head groundsman at Trent Bridge, and his crew have produced some absolutely belting wickets for one-day cricket in recent years and this one was up among the best.

It was the start of a crazy few weeks at the ground when it was like bowling on glass, as it simply didn't offer anything for the bowlers at all.

The ball came on to the bat so well it was almost impossible to keep any of the batsmen quiet. Add in the lightning fast outfield and small boundaries and there's no wonder that we saw some stupidly high scores.

Michael Lumb and Riki Wessels set the tone, each smashing huge hundreds after putting on 342 for the first wicket, as we made our way to 445/8.

It's worth bearing in mind that that total was the second highest ever recorded in one-day cricket at the time. I say that because at times we thought that it might not be enough as Northants pushed us close.

Rory Kleinveldt, Northants' powerful South African all-rounder, had torn his side and his quad and was batting with a runner but just kept belting it everywhere.

I thought, 'Jeez, we're in bother here.'

He blazed his way to 128 from 63 balls but then hit one up in the air off me and was caught at cow corner by Anuj Dal.

They scored 425 and lost, that's how ridiculous that day was!

30

Taunton Torments

WHILE STILL new to county cricket, I quickly learned that if you are going to have any success against Somerset then you need to remove Marcus Trescothick fairly cheaply.

The left-handed opener had been something of a hero of mine as I cheered him on during the 2005 Ashes series.

A fabulous player to watch on television, he's quite a daunting one to face out in the middle. Little did I think, when I first played against him, that we would get to know each other well over the years and become mates.

One season, soon after I'd started, I had a spot of good fortune when playing against him and managed to get him out a few times, which I was delighted about.

We had a lad with us at Notts called Neil Edwards, who had signed for the county from Somerset. His time at Trent Bridge coincided with his wedding down in the west country somewhere and players from both counties were in attendance.

As usual at such an event, a few beers were taken and then after a glass or two of wine you start to get a bit 'confident', don't you?

I went to the bar and Marcus was there, waiting to be served. It was too good an opportunity to resist.

'Hi Marcus,' I said. 'Are you going to take a leg stump guard when we play you next year?'

He looked at me quizzically and said, 'What are you on about?'

I was up for this now. 'Are you going to take a leg stump guard next year?'

'Why?' he enquired.

The next sentence seemed really funny to me as the words left my mouth. 'Because I'm sick of hitting you on the pads.'

He stared at me and said nothing. There was a pause that seemed like an hour. I began to wonder if he'd heard me.

Then something happened that took me completely by surprise. He headbutted me.

A million thoughts went through my head about how I should react but the overriding one was of pride, pride at being headbutted by an Ashes hero!

It certainly broke the ice between us and we chatted and found we got along pretty well. I have to say our on-field battles over the years have always been pretty intense but there's usually been some fun involved, as Marcus would testify.

* * *

Marcus Trescothick: 'We've had a great relationship over the years and I've always enjoyed having a laugh with Fletch.

'It all stemmed from that wedding, where we both ended up head-butting each other – jokingly, don't let him tell you it was anything different!

'I don't know why I was doing it though, he's got the hardest head around.

'He's such a good bloke and so well regarded within the game; just a legend of a man.

'On the field he's so funny and when he tries to be anything different and be grumpy it makes it even funnier. You just can't take him seriously.

'One time we were out on the field and got chatting about our favourite types of chocolate. We were both in agreement that peanut M&Ms take some beating.

'It became a bit of a tradition after then that whenever our paths crossed, we'd each arrive with a bag for the other one.

'Fletch's humour shouldn't take anything away from his ability because he really is a decent bowler. Six or seven years ago, when Trent Bridge was fairly lively, we had some great battles. He would consistently hit good areas and always managed to find the right zone.

'Batsmen have to give him a lot of respect because he's such a tough opponent.

'One year we played at Notts in the T20 quarter-finals and he really surprised me by bowling accurate yorkers with the new ball.

'I'd knackered my foot in the warm-ups and just couldn't get him away. In the end, trying to do something differently, I got out scooping him straight to short fine leg.

'More recently I'll know whenever he's on a big night out because I'll get some random text message from him at all hours of the night!'

* * *

Marcus and his Somerset side broke Nottinghamshire hearts two years running in the T20. They beat us at the Rose Bowl on Finals Day in 2010 and were then well on their way to knocking us out at Trent Bridge a year later, when I had a bit of a run-in with Kieron Pollard.

It was a quarter-final match, televised live on Sky Sports, and the ground was packed to the rafters. We scored 169/5 and looked in good order until Pollard and Jos Buttler joined forces.

The all-rounder was going along nicely and we knew we had to get him out to have any chance.

Buttler was still fairly young but was starting to make his mark in the game and began doing these cute little scoop shots, really pi**ing us off.

Pollard was loving it at the other end, carrying on, strutting around and generally being a bit of a t**t.

It was my turn to bowl at Pollard. I wanted to get him out so badly and brought my short fine leg up and delivered a near-perfect yorker.

Sadly for me the big West Indian jabbed his bat down on it at the last second and got a fortuitous bottom edge past the stumps and away for four.

It really pushed my buttons. Having thought I'd absolutely nailed it, he was just grinning at me instead, really lapping it up.

Giving him the glare from close quarters I stupidly called him a spawny c**t, not the sort of language I'd normally resort to.

It clearly riled him because, as I was walking back to my mark, he deliberately shoulder barged me. Pollard is a big lad and I'm a big lad and it wouldn't have made good viewing for those watching, either in the ground or on television as it developed into a bit of a pushing and shoving spat.

He had the last laugh, of course, and celebrated loudly after guiding Somerset over the line and through to Finals Day.

That night, the worse for wear and feeling pretty down, I was out with Darren Bravo, who was with Notts at the time and is a Trinidad and West Indies teammate of Pollard's.

We got talking about what had happened and how he'd got to me when Bravo mentioned that he'd got Pollard's number.

I took his phone and rang the number. To this day I can't remember what I said but it wasn't complimentary. It was an idiotic thing to do but he took it surprisingly well and laughed it off.

Pollard is a big unit and I thought afterwards, 'Jeez, what have I done? He's built like a bus.'

Bravo told me later that he'd spoken to his mate and all was forgotten. I've not seen Pollard since but I've decided that I'll never spray him again if our paths ever cross!

* * *

Chris Read also recalls one embarrassing moment for me in a match against Somerset at Taunton: 'Umpires across the country had started having a crackdown on players leaving the field, bowlers just nipping off whenever the mood suited them.

'Fletch had left it a bit late to go to the toilet during the tea break and the bell sounded for us to get back out there.

'I wanted him to bowl the first over after the restart but he wasn't ready and told us so from his cubicle.

'It took some yelling but he made it on to the field just in time to begin bowling. During the over, though, he announced that he needed to go off at the end of it.

'The umpires were quickly all over it. "You should have gone in the break," they said.

'His response? "I did – but I haven't wiped up properly!"'

31

Smacked Like A Fish

IN JULY 2013 we were playing against Surrey at The Oval and at the same time England were playing a Test against Australia at Trent Bridge.

This was Ricky Ponting's final game of professional cricket. The former Aussie skipper was hanging up his boots after 20 years in the sport.

I was excited about perhaps being the last bloke to ever get Ricky Ponting out, so the night before I was absolutely buzzing.

We rocked up to the ground the next morning and I received the news that I'd been left out of our starting XI. I was spewing with anger and disappointment – I really wasn't very happy because I knew that this would have been my only chance to bowl at Ponting.

Having calmed down later I looked at the positives and thought I'd at least get a chance to have a bit of a chat with him.

Surrey were batting, Ponting was in the middle and I was 12th man. A wicket was taken at the other end, so I ran out with the drinks and dished them out to our lads.

Then I made my way down to the Vauxhall End, where the former Aussie skipper was standing.

'Hey, your lot are struggling at Trent Bridge,' I offered as an opener.

'You what?'

'Your lot are struggling, you want to get yourself in a taxi and get up there,' I encouraged.

'You f***ing what? Why don't you get off the f***ing pitch, you fat f***er?'

He was practically shouting at me.

With it being a county game there wasn't much noise around to prevent everyone from hearing him give me this volley.

I could feel my face getting redder and redder and all my teammates and the two umpires were laughing at me. It wasn't my intention to abuse him, all I'd wanted to do was speak to a cricketing great.

Ponting didn't stop there. 'Who the f**k are you anyway? Look at the state of you, no wonder you can't get in the f***ing team.'

Andre Adams was lapping it up, watching from the other end, and now recalls, 'Punter [Ponting] really tore a strip off Fletch, he smacked him like a fish. When he started calling him a fat c**t I thought I'd better step in.

'"Come on Punter, he's only being friendly." The Australian wasn't having any of it. "Nah, he was being a dick."'

Thankfully the drinks break was over and it was time for me to get out of there. So off the field I walked, feeling well and truly chastised. Mick Newell was waiting for me and had witnessed the exchange. He asked what had gone off but when I told him he started laying into me for being so bloody stupid!

I've not been anywhere near Ponting since but a few years later Graeme Swann was working with him on the radio and brought that incident up. They both had a good laugh about it and Swanny sent me a WhatsApp message with Ricky apologising for being so hard on me!

* * *

I had to smile when Surrey won the County Championship title in 2018 for the first time in ages because of something their director of cricket said.

I've always regarded Alec Stewart as an absolute legend, both as a cricketer and as a bloke, and he was understandably delighted when his troops deservedly lifted the title.

During one of many post-event interviews he came out with a cracking line, which I've repeated for my own amusement ever since. Explaining how he'd built his formidable squad he revealed, 'It's been a three-year plan.'

Allow me a spot of indulgence here because three years earlier, I wasn't getting much of a look-in at Notts and was allowed to go on loan to Surrey.

* * *

Alec Stewart: 'I've always had a lot of time for Fletch and was delighted to be able to bring him to Surrey for a short spell in 2015.

'At the time we had a few injuries and were a little short of bowlers. I needed someone – and this isn't a criticism – who was an old-fashioned type of bowler, someone like Angus Fraser used to be, who can run in all day and hit the top of off repeatedly.

'The game revolves around the top of off stump and my homework suggested that he was that sort of player, someone who doesn't get too fancy and is someone you can reply on.

'There's not enough consistency in the game but Fletch thrives on it.

'He had a big impact on our side, particularly through his character but also through his level of performance, showing our bowlers what can happen when you are consistent.

'If he'd been out of contract or if Nottinghamshire had agreed to let him go, I'd have happily signed him. That's probably the biggest credit I can pay him.

'There is a sort of outside perception of Surrey and many may wonder what it's like playing for the county. But he really got us straightaway. He enjoyed us and we enjoyed having him around.'

* * *

I've never minded Surrey as a club but just wish they weren't based in south London because it's always a pain in the a**e to get to.

It's horrendous. Whenever I have played at The Oval, over the years, we have always stayed in a hotel about two miles away and it has still taken about 40 minutes to get there.

Not that it was a concern during my brief loan spell with the club. I played three matches for them, all away from The Oval; visiting Northampton, Beckenham and Derby.

Kumar Sangakkara was their overseas player at the time and he was very welcoming. In truth, I found it a great changing room and quickly formed some good friendships there.

Alec Stewart was top class. I don't think he's ever actually come out and said that I was his best signing but I'm sure that's what he meant!

32

It's Always Uphill

THERE'S NOT much to beat a trip to Hove, especially when the weather is good. Usually we stay close enough to be able to have a stroll along the seafront on our way to the ground.

Mind you, it's another place where I've struggled to get to grips with the slope. The first time I played there, with England under-19s, I had a bit of success running up the hill.

Whether that has clouded my opinion or not, I can't be sure, but ever since I've really not taken to the other end, the Cromwell Road End.

I've always bowled s**t from there and just not been able to get it right. It always feels like I'm getting ahead of myself and get my timing all wrong coming downhill.

Andre Adams always used to say the same thing about bowling there but Harry Gurney will have other feelings, I'm sure.

I was stood at mid-off the year that Harry got a hat-trick at Hove and couldn't have been more delighted for him. A genuinely lovely lad, it's always good to be able to share in a teammate's success.

One of the most ruthless victories I've been involved in came against Sussex, when we beat them inside two days at Trent Bridge in 2017.

On the second day we made them follow on and then dismissed Sussex cheaply for a second time, picking up 17 wickets inside the three sessions.

Our quartet of fast bowlers, Stuart Broad, James Pattinson, Jake Ball and myself, were all on song at the same time and the Sussex batsmen looked like rabbits in the headlights as we tore through them. Harry missed that match but around that time, I felt our five quicker bowlers were as good a unit as any around.

* * *

My former Nottinghamshire teammate Ali Brown has always been a big fan of greyhound racing and one year, when we were playing down at Hove, he sorted us all out with some tickets to go down to the local track there. Even though I was on my very best behaviour throughout, somehow I still became the centre of attention.

* * *

Ali Brown: 'A friend of mine, Simon Clare, head of PR at Coral, managed to sort us out with some tables, so the whole squad, including Stuart Broad and Graeme Swann, went down to enjoy the evening together.

'The favourite for the feature race, the Olympic Final, was called Blonde Fletch, so naturally we were all over it.

'We all decided to back it, even though it was priced at 4/6 on, and agreed we would celebrate like we had won the lottery if it came in first – all in honour of our own Blonde Fletch!

'The dog duly romped home and we all went crazy, even though none of us had won more than £20. I think from the noise we were making everyone assumed we had taken the stadium down with a massive win!'

33

'Yeah, No Worries Fletch!'

ONE OF my most embarrassing moments on a cricket field came in a home four-day match against Warwickshire and it involved Samit Patel.

He's played cricket for a long time but you wouldn't know it sometimes because, on occasions, he doesn't appear to have a clue what he's doing.

Time and time again he's shown what a wonderfully talented cricketer he is and he's a great lad to be around, but he's had his moments!

On this particular day things hadn't gone well. Warwickshire had racked up a sizeable score, with Ian Bell getting his usual ton against us.

They'd then used the rest of the day to scythe through our top order, leaving us at 36/5 when L.J. Fletcher wandered out into the evening gloom as nightwatchman.

To be fair to the Nottinghamshire members, they have always given me a tremendous reception whenever I've gone out to bat, but the collapse of those five quick wickets had already aroused the boo-boys.

There were quite a few cries of dissent at the sight of their big fast bowler coming out to bat in such circumstances and with only five minutes left in the day nothing was going to send them home to a cheery supper.

You'll have your own views on the wisdom of nightwatchmen and cricket is full of instances of them transforming the course of a contest. On this occasion my job was to protect the next batsman due to come in. In this case it was Chris Read.

Quite simply, I just needed to be on strike for the last over. If I got out then, well it's not ideal but it meant that Chris could join Samit in the morning.

Clearly, given the state of the contest, I wasn't looking to get out as we headed for the final over of the day.

I was on strike and said to Samit, 'I'll face the first two or three balls and if there's the chance to run a two then we will, otherwise stay where you are.

'I need to stay at this end, so even numbers or nothing. You don't need to be on strike. Understand?'

'Yeah, no worries Fletch,' he muttered.

They had an attacking field, pressing for another wicket. I pushed the ball out into the deep. There was the easiest two you could imagine – we could probably have run four if we'd needed to.

Anyway, for reasons best known to him, after completing the easy two Samit came bombing back towards me for a third run.

I yelled for him to go back but to no avail, we were both at the same end and I was honour-bound to give up my wicket.

'I told you not to do that,' I said, as the booing started.

Head down, we all trooped off towards the pavilion as one lone voice summed up the mood, shouting, 'You useless fat bastard,' but I wasn't sure which one of us he was addressing.

* * *

I once had a stumping off my bowling and it came against Warwickshire. It's not usually very flattering for a quick (or even a medium-paced trundler) to revel in the wicketkeeper standing up to you, unless that gloveman is Chris Read.

The occasion was a one-dayer at Trent Bridge that went down to the very last ball of the contest. There was plenty riding on it as well; lose and we would be out but win and we would secure a home quarter-final.

My one and only (as far as I can remember) stumping in county cricket was a fairly routine one, it has to be said. Rikki Clarke came towards me and missed it, leaving Readie to do the rest.

Figures of 4-44 were my one-day best at the time but the Bears still posted a challenging score of 302/7.

We had it all to do. I was hoping to relax and watch our top order do their thing but it was a nervy watch. Baz scored his usual century against Warwickshire but we still needed more than 100 when he got out.

Wickets fell regularly and we needed 20 from 12 balls when I made my way out to the middle. Ajmal Shahzad was run out in the final over, leaving just myself and last man Harry Gurney to try and get us over the line.

The scores were nudged level, leaving me on strike against Oliver Hannon-Dalby for the final delivery. I've rarely felt such a rush of euphoria as I punched his full-pitched delivery back past him and down the ground for four to seal the one-wicket win and qualification for the next round.

There was a fair bit of bat-twirling and back-slapping as I made my way off the field, basking in one of the best moments of my career.

34

Gangly And Bony

AMONG THE photographs in this book you'll perhaps have noticed one of myself and Stuart Broad having a 'coming together' in full cricket gear.

It occurred during a game against Worcestershire at New Road and ended up with us both going down for the full ten count.

You've heard of ball watching? I'm not even sure if that was to blame. Basically, neither of us were looking where we were going after he hit one out to long-on.

From memory, I think we must have been looking for two runs because I had my head down, running hard. He was doing the same.

It was the perfect recipe for disaster and we must have looked like a pair of rutting stags (quite fitting, given the county motif on our shirts at the time) as we charged into each other.

We both went down in a heap, felled like two giant redwoods. Self-preservation kicked in and we both somehow scrambled back to our respective ends before going down again.

He'd whacked me hard, properly belted me and stuck his elbow into my ribs. But the pretty boy had ended up with a cut nose, so had all of the physio's attention.

* * *

Stuart Broad: 'I think we were both looking where the ball was and there was no hint or tip that we were going to run into each other but we did.

'Being run into by Fletch isn't something I'd want to experience every day. I can only imagine it's like being hit by a train or a heavyweight boxer. My chinstrap moved as his metal visor slammed into my face.

'He knocked the sense out of me and judging by that collision Fletch could have made it as an NFL star.

'There was only me had the concussion test afterwards, so you can tell who came off worse.

'The noise of the impact will always stay with me but also the noise made by the Worcestershire wicketkeeper Ben Cox, who made a gasp of disbelief at the collision.'

* * *

Thankfully, neither of us was badly hurt and I suppose it must have looked quite funny to everyone else.

I did learn something though. Broady is quite a bony man. You know those tall, gangly, bony people? Yes, he's one of them. Horrible.

* * *

One of the most extraordinary County Championship matches I've played in was at New Road against Worcestershire. More often than not, if you lose a full day of cricket you will struggle to get a positive result.

So it's not surprising that if both of the first two days are totally washed away then it's almost unheard of for either side to force a win.

Rain at New Road isn't unheard of, of course. We've all seen the photographs of the ground frequently being flooded and felt for the ground staff who always do such a sterling job to get it playable again.

In 2018 we travelled to Worcester and feared the worst. The weather forecast for the first two days was awful and if the ground got a really bad soaking then it may have prevented any play being possible.

As anticipated, it chucked it down for 48 hours but then things began to improve. We stuck them in at the start of the third day and were batting by lunch.

Broady and Jake Ball had reduced the home side to 3/3. I came on and found a decent length on my way to career-best figures of 5-27. We built a good lead and I even whacked a few (27 not out) before skittling Worcestershire again on the last day. A four-day championship match done in just over four sessions!

* * *

Poor old bowlers. We rarely get the accolades that are dished out to batsmen but on one occasion I unexpectedly won a man of the match award in a televised game.

It was early on in my career and came after a T20 clash against Worcestershire at New Road, a low-scoring affair that we scraped through. I only took one wicket but didn't go for many runs and was announced as the recipient.

David 'Bumble' Lloyd made the presentation and interviewed me on the outfield. I was fairly naïve at the time and my cricket knowledge wasn't the greatest.

'You reminded me of Angus Fraser,' said the famous commentator.

I'm sure he wasn't expecting me to reply with, 'Who?'

Sorry Gus!

* * *

There was a match against Worcestershire that heralded a new phrase between Stuart Broad and myself, as the England international recalls: 'Playing against them in a day-nighter at Trent Bridge I was about to bowl a bouncer to Ross Whiteley.

'Looking around the field I realised I'd got Fletch at mid-on and Harry Gurney at square leg. Not ideal, I thought and asked if they'd care to swap over for me.

'In his usual laid-back manner Fletch said, "Ah, we'll be all right," effectively telling me that he couldn't be bothered moving the 15 yards or so that I wanted him to.

'Predictably the ball went straight up in the air, towards square leg. Harry struggled to get underneath it and didn't even lay a mitt on it.

'There was a moment's silence. It's always an uncomfortable time when a chance goes begging like that and I looked towards Fletch.

'Now, we both know that he hasn't dropped it but also we both know that I'd wanted him to go there and if he had done he would have caught it. He's always had good hands and would definitely have held the catch.

'It wasn't his fault but if he'd walked the 15 yards I'd wanted him to we'd all have been better off.

'The ball is thrown to him and he walks towards me, saying as he hands it over, "It's one of them!"

'I didn't necessarily agree, "It's not one of them Fletch, it's the furthest from one of them it could be."

'He has this knack of being able to defuse any situation and that is now our way of communicating whenever a chance goes down.

'We'll look at each other and one of us will just say, "It's one of them!"'

35

A Cacophony Of Boos

SOME OF my most memorable contests against Yorkshire have come when we've played them at their picturesque ground at North Marine Road, Scarborough. I remember one year in particular when, during a 50-over match, I came in for quite a bit of stick.

The ground was packed and there was a cracking atmosphere. It's a place where you feel the spectators are right on top of you and it can feel quite intimidating at times.

I chased a ball down towards the pavilion boundary and put a bit of a slide in. I've no idea if I dragged it back in time or not as I slid into the rope but the umpires took me at my word and only three runs were awarded instead of four.

The crowd went potty, calling me all the names under the sun. I always enjoy a bit of banter with spectators but they gave it to me in buckets, calling me a cheat, as well as plenty of uncomplimentary comments about my build.

Cricket never seems to let incidents like that subside quietly and the barracking got louder and louder as the ball kept coming to me.

Throughout the course of the innings four Yorkshire batsmen decided to hit the ball high towards me. On each occasion, to a cacophony of boos, I managed to take the catch, celebrating more and more enthusiastically each time.

They'd obviously forgiven me by the time I took a five-wicket haul there in 2019. I'd had to bowl quite a long spell and was eventually rewarded.

I think it's the only time I've walked off to a standing ovation from opposition fans. Fair play, they were excellent to me that day and it's one of the proudest moments of my career as I led our side off the field.

* * *

In stark contrast to being booed on the field, it's always nice to hear your own fans getting behind you. Some grounds retain the atmosphere better than others and Trent Bridge is certainly high on that list.

I guess it's a little difficult to equate what has been the loudest I've ever heard the Notts supporters get on our home turf but they were simply unbelievable for a T20 Blast win over Yorkshire in 2019.

Winning is always that much sweeter when you've played a part yourself and I felt that I contributed a little bit towards an incredible victory that evening.

Admittedly, a score of only six with the bat and bowling figures of 2-31 don't look that special on paper but a spot of context can improve them no end.

I went out to the middle in the final over of our innings and got on strike with just two deliveries remaining. Both were clubbed away; the first for six and the second into the hands of long-on.

A strike rate of 300, folks! The significance of my six and out became very relevant later.

We needed to win that match to secure our passage through to the knockout phase but the visitors chased hard throughout and needed just 18 from the remaining two overs of their innings.

I was entrusted to bowl the 19th over. All you are really looking to do is make sure that you keep your side in it. Concede as few as possible and hope you can force a mistake or two from them.

The many hours I've spent nailing my yorkers paid off handsomely in that over as I splattered the stumps of Jack Leaning and Tim Bresnan, while conceding only six runs.

I'd done my bit and, without exaggeration, I'd not heard our supporters ever be as loud as that before, as they roared us on.

With just 12 needed from the final over, the match looked to be going away from us as Will Fraine hit Harry Gurney's first ball for six.

Back came Gurney though, first with a wicket and then with a succession of deliveries that totally bamboozled the opposition as we sealed the win. I played my part in that final over as well, pulling off a full-length diving sprawl at short fine leg to stop a boundary.

The noise was immense and that was an evening that will stay with me forever.

36

Celebrations

FOR AS long as cricket has been played, bowlers have enjoyed taking wickets but pre-orchestrated celebrations have been somewhat lacking in our sport, compared to what we see elsewhere.

You only have to look at American football, for instance, to witness what goes off after a touchdown.

How much time do they spend practicing their art on the training ground and how much time is spent rehearsing their celebration routine?

Cricket, thankfully, has not quite got to those levels across the board yet, although there have been a few individuals who have done it 'their way'.

Australia's Brett Lee, one of the fastest bowlers the game has ever seen, had his own particular trademark, 'The Chainsaw Celebration', allegedly done as a tribute to his dad after spending hours watching him cut up wood as a youngster.

Lee played a pivotal role in that amazing 2005 Ashes series, when arguably Freddie Flintoff was at his best. Freddie's own spread-eagled crucifix impression is another lasting memory from that great summer.

The quicks don't have it all their own way when it comes to flamboyant celebrations. A couple of South African spin bowlers always provide good value whenever they take a wicket.

Imran Tahir, who has played for at least half a dozen English counties, including Notts, takes some catching whenever he strikes. Off he goes, on a joyous run to wherever the fancy takes him, leaving teammates in his wake.

It doesn't seem to bother Tahir if he's got out the world's best player or a complete rabbit. As soon as he hits the stumps or sees the umpire's finger go up, he's off. Catch him if you can.

His international teammate Tabraiz Shamsi has begun to introduce a new jeopardy to celebrating. For a while the left-arm wrist spinner would whip off one of his cricket shoes, hold it up as a mobile phone, dial away on the studs and pretend he was making a call.

In itself, that seemed a bit whacky but now Shamsi has taken things on to a very different level. During his younger days he fancied himself as a bit of a magician.

Presumably one Christmas he got a magic set instead of the Subbuteo Cricket he was expecting.

He clearly learnt a few things and still remembers one or two of his tricks. During the South Africa Super League

T20 he was playing for his team, Paarl Rocks, when he took a wicket.

'Magic Sham' whipped a red handkerchief out of his pocket and, quick as a flash, turned it into a magic wand. Mightily impressive indeed. The world wonders what he might do next. Sawing a teammate in half? Making an umpire disappear?

Clearly I'll have to up my game from now on.

There are all sorts of ways in which a bowler can get a wicket and lots of things that can influence your reaction when it happens.

I don't have a standard way of celebrating, although there are plenty of photos of me around raising a clenched right fist, so I guess that must be an involuntary response to striking lucky.

There's also the regulation both arms raised pose, like on the front cover of this book. But occasionally, like all other bowlers, I guess I can go over the top a little.

Anything could lead to that. Perhaps you've had three or four decisions go against you and it's a show of relief, or maybe you're just so happy because it's an important wicket for the team to get at that time (when is a wicket not important?).

Sometimes the sheer magnitude of the player you've got out can also play a part – I know I've always enjoyed getting the opposition's 'star' man out.

There are also other factors that might influence your reaction. In 2015 Notts had let me go to Surrey on loan for the first month of the season.

My return to Trent Bridge coincided with the start of that year's T20 Blast competition. I was included for the opener, a match to be televised live at home against Birmingham Bears, the defending champions.

I was under no illusions that this was a big moment in my career.

There were over 10,000 in the ground and the atmosphere was electric. Harry Gurney, Jake Ball and Vernon Philander all had a bowl before I was brought on.

The Notts fans have always been brilliant to me and I was a little concerned that things might have changed with me having been off the scene for a while.

Those thoughts were quickly dispelled as they roared their approval as my name was announced over the tannoy.

Nevertheless, I was a little nervous as I ran in to bowl. Tim Ambrose was on strike. Full and straight, full and straight Fletch.

The cricketing gods were on my side as a textbook yorker speared into the batsman's middle stump. Trent Bridge erupted – they must have heard the noise in the city centre.

I was delighted, a release of energy, an outpouring of emotion. I was back and didn't care who knew it. I ran around like a lunatic and disappeared under a pile of Outlaws.

The hairs on the back of my neck were standing upright. I'm not sure where Cloud Nine is but I was on it!

I was pumped full of adrenaline and high on emotion but had I paused to think, then the reality was that there was probably only one way I could go now after that start.

Only I didn't!

I repeated an exact same delivery to york Rikki Clarke in the same over and then did it again in my last to dismiss Laurie Evans, giving me figures of 3-24.

It had been a decent comeback for me but I've always been about the team first and the most important thing was to win the match.

I needn't have worried as Alex Hales put on a show for the TV cameras. At one stage he hit sixes from six consecutive deliveries (facing three from each end), on his way to a rapid 86 not out from only 43 balls.

It had been an early finish, thanks to my mate Baz and not for the first time he was soon on the outfield collecting the man-of-the-match champagne.

Celebrating isn't just for bowlers either. There aren't many better sights on a cricket field than watching the reaction of players when a teammate pulls off an absolute worldy of a catch.

Watching normally sane individuals go bonkers at seeing something outrageous is one of the great joys of the game. Players are just fans at heart and if we see something astonishing then it's only normal that we'll react in the same way.

By and large batting has been a painful experience for me, one way or another, and hasn't provided too many highs but every few years along comes a chance for me to hit the winning runs.

The most remarkable occasion, I guess, was in a T20 Blast match against Lancashire at Trent Bridge. They'd scored a healthy 184/4 and when I arrived at the crease in the penultimate over, to join Sam Wood, we were in a bit of a pickle.

I scratched a single somewhere to get off the mark but it meant that we still required a further 15 runs from the final six deliveries.

I'm not sure what the odds would have been on an Outlaws victory at that stage but let's say I was hopeful, more than glowingly optimistic.

Then things changed in our favour quite rapidly.

Lancashire hadn't managed to bowl their overs in the pre-requisite time, so were penalised six runs. The equation was now just nine needed from six balls.

Arron Lilley, a right-arm off-spinner, was given the ball. I forced another single and sat back in admiration as Woody launched the ball high into the New Stand for six.

He nudged a run to bring the scores level and that left me on strike with three deliveries left. The turnaround had been sudden and dramatic and I just needed a bit of composure to finish the job off.

It wasn't the most elegant run I've ever scored – I went to play it through the off side and dragged it with a thick inside-edge down to deep square leg.

Running towards the pavilion I could see our fans all rise together to celebrate victory. It was an exhilarating moment and not one I was used to.

Milking the moment, I completed most of the run with my bat held aloft, twirling it round jubilantly like I'd won the World Cup.

I was pleased for Sam Wood, there's no doubt that the six he'd hit had been the game-clincher but the beam on my face told its own story.

Returning to my back-slapping teammates I had a rare vision of what it must be like to be someone like Hales or Samit.

Is hitting the winning runs a better feeling than getting the final wicket in a close game?

Nah!

37

Clean Hitting

I CAN'T really complain about the number of opportunities I've had in red-ball cricket to show what I can do with the bat.

Often enough I've been out there at number eight or nine, against a softish ball and in ideal conditions. I've also had my fair share of nightwatchman duties, so I've had my chances to impress in the longer format.

Perhaps that's not always been the case in the shorter formats though. I've only ever been sent out at nine, ten or 11 with an over or so to go and instructions to 'get down the other end' and leave it to Samit or Mull or Readie.

I've always been able to hold a bat and I do work hard on my skills. Over the last couple of years that has started to pay off, I think.

In the 2018 quarter-final I hit 53 not out from 34 balls against Kent and the following season I produced some of the cleanest hitting of my career.

We played an extraordinary match against Lancashire at Trent Bridge, with both sides scoring over 400.

Joe Clarke had scored a quite brilliant hundred for us and we had pounded their attack in reaching 349/5 when I was sent in with four overs to go.

Matt Parkinson, Lancashire's young leg-spinner, has since gone on to play for England and has a very bright future in the game but I've done pretty well whenever I've come up against him.

The previous year I'd hit him for a big six at Old Trafford and with runs on the board I had a free licence to throw the bat and see how many I could add to our imposing total.

From the 17 balls I faced I managed to club my way to 46 not out, hitting five sixes and two fours. Parkinson received the worst treatment, as I hit him for four maximums within the space of five balls, throwing a four in the mix for good measure as I took 28 from one over.

With Trent Bridge living up to its billing as one of the best grounds for one-day cricket, Lancashire gave it a real go themselves and came within a whisker of chasing down our 417/7.

Centuries from Steven Croft and Dane Vilas had them in the box seat for much of the chase until James Pattinson's five wickets brought us a nervy 11-run victory.

While that was the most sustained piece of clean hitting I've produced at county level I didn't have long to wait before I added distance to my cv.

Just four days after that Lancashire match we went to Edgbaston and my juices were still flowing when I went out, again with a licence to cut loose.

I hit one from Alex Thomson that sailed away, high, high, high and over the Hollies Stand. It's difficult to confirm really but I think that must be the biggest blow I've ever connected with.

Of course, there's that saying, 'what goes around comes around', and I've been on the wrong end of a few as well.

The top tier of the Radcliffe Road End at Trent Bridge is quite a decent hit and Jos Buttler once put me right on the very top of that, it almost went over.

There's not a lot that a bowler can say in those situations, you just have to do better next time, or in Buttler's case get him off strike!

Buttler's former Somerset teammate Craig Kieswetter also went 'large' against me, putting me on top of the retirement apartments at Taunton.

38

County Cap

IT'S ALWAYS a proud moment for any cricketer when they receive their county cap. I had to wait quite a while before getting mine, mainly due to all the off-field issues that kept being mentioned to the committee I guess.

The awarding of a cap is done differently at each county but at Trent Bridge it's the committee who approve the award, presumably after a consultation with the director of cricket or head coach. Thankfully, they ensure certain standards are maintained and the recipient has the desired professionalism they are looking for.

As I alluded to, they kept me waiting until 2014, by which time I'd amassed 175 first-class wickets for them.

Notts also issue a county cap to anyone on the staff who is selected for full international honours. With Harry Gurney having played his first match for England, we were all aware that a presentation was imminent but leaving the field at lunch on the first day of a home match against Middlesex provided a shock I wasn't expecting. I noticed Kirsty there – and then her father as well. Both had cameras. Mick Newell had contacted them and it had all been kept from me and I hadn't twigged at all.

Not only were Harry and I being capped but Riki Wessels was as well. I assume there was a job lot going; buy three Notts caps for the price of one.

Being capped made so much difference to me. There was a few extra quid in the pay packet but it wasn't about that. I actually felt like I'd achieved something; it had been a massive goal to be capped and it was now confirmation that I'd achieved the necessary consistency in my game.

I was so proud. I'd never lost the thrill of representing Nottinghamshire, my home county, but now it had been taken on to a new level.

That said, the cap didn't remain new for very long. I only have to bowl two or three balls, whatever the weather, and I'm sweating.

My county cap has been in a few scrapes and had a few things tipped over it and, for something I love so much, it's not really been looked after very well.

At the end of each cricket season it gets stuffed into an inside pocket in my cricket bag and is left to stiffen up for about five months each winter.

It always comes out about five sizes too small and it always takes two or three matches before it fits again.

Like in the best traditions of the Aussie baggy greens, I'd never dream of having my cap dry-cleaned, so with all the continuous forehead perspiration inside it, it doesn't smell too sweet. It looks like it should be 400 games old, not just over 100.

Some of the umpires aren't too keen on it at all. Jeff Evans refuses to touch it, full stop. He carries a little plastic bag around, which he holds open and waits for me to pop the cap inside.

Several others insist I leave it down at fine-leg or long-leg when I'm bowling. A few have told me that only Steve Harmison's smelled worse.

My sweater also comes in for quite a lot of criticism as well, big, heavy and smelly. It's a good job I have a decent relationship with the umpires.

* * *

Steve Garratt: 'As an umpire you dreaded Fletch bowling from your end on a hot day. He has what could best be described as a high perspiration level, the sweat just pours out of him. Holding his cap and sweater was always a challenging experience!

'But Fletch was always one of the umpire's first picks for our nice guys XI. I would always greet him with the phrase, "Ay up Fletch, how's your front foot today?" A testament to his penchant for bowling no-balls.'

* * *

There were plenty of occasions early on in my career when I did struggle with no-balls but most umpires are very good about it. They'll give you a bit of a warning if you're close to over-stepping, 'Pull it back lad, you're tramming it [getting close] this morning.'

It's usually when I'm running in hard, really committing that I may fall foul of the rule but as I get more tired towards the end of a long day I perhaps don't quite run in as hard and it's no longer a problem.

39

Mooresy

I'VE BEEN very fortunate in working with some of the very best coaches in the game. Peter Moores certainly fits in to that category and since taking over first team affairs from Mick Newell at the end of the 2016 season he has had a massive impact on my career. He's definitely one of the hardest-working coaches around and has helped so much with my batting, in particular. He probably spends as much time with the lower-order batters as with the top order and has significantly improved certain aspects of my game, as well as giving me the confidence to go out and deliver in those areas.

As a head coach he had already achieved great success before coming to Trent Bridge, having won the County Championship with Sussex and Lancashire, as well as having two spells in charge of England.

His magic touch hadn't deserted him, as Notts won two white-ball trophies and a promotion in his first season in charge at Trent Bridge.

Mooresy knew how much it meant to me to play in that Lord's final against Surrey and he was on hand a week later when my world threatened to fall apart at Edgbaston.

* * *

Peter Moores: 'It's very easy for me to remember Luke's reaction at being selected for the final because I knew what a boost it would be, both for him and for the rest of the team.

'He talked about getting Jason Roy out – he was so confident he'd get him – and it would have worked if we hadn't shelled that chance first ball of the match.

'It turned into a special day for us all and I can remember Luke showing me a photo that had been taken of his son Freddie touching the television screen, as if to say, "Look, that's my dad and he's playing in a Lord's final."

'Then, one week later. Nobody will ever be able to forget what happened at Edgbaston. In a way it was always going to happen to someone in the modern game because we know how hard batsmen hit the ball and there's such little reaction time for a bowler to get out of the way.

'We knew it was bad from the noise it made, it was such a sickening sound as the ball struck him.

'It was a tough day, not only for Luke but for everyone else as well and it wasn't nice to see him like that, a bloodied towel round his head, oxygen mask on. The lads were in bits but typically, Luke was more bothered about them and kept putting his thumbs up to reassure them he was all right.

'He is arguably one of the best team men I've ever coached, he's got this brilliant openness about him as a person. There's no edge to him, he loves the game. He commits to it and loves to compete and get stuck in.

'And he drags people along with him and brings the best out of everyone. We quickly noticed that when he was fielding at mid-off Patto [James Pattinson] would always bowl much better.

'Luke keeps things nicely in perspective. It's still a game, remember, whether you're playing on the village green or out in the middle at Trent Bridge and you will always play your best cricket if you are still able to relax when the pressure is on.

'He's a catalyst for others to do well and what I've enjoyed most about him, as a coach, is that he's gone on again to the next level. You expect youngsters to constantly strive to improve but since his late 20s he has added something to his game each year.

'Luke will look on with great satisfaction at what he's achieved and he'll do it with a smile on his face because that's how he always is.'

* * *

The thing that mostly stands out about Mooresy is that he likes to work hard and play hard.

One of the best days of my life was organised by him towards the end of a pre-season tour to Barbados.

The lads had really put in a shift throughout the time we were there and on the last day the coach arranged for all the squad to go out on to the Caribbean Sea in a catamaran.

There's no funny stories attached to this, no stand-out individual moment. It was just a brilliant day that he sorted out from start to finish, as a way to wind down and relax together.

Not all team-bonding days have been as enjoyable as that one though. One year the club organised a paint-balling day for players and club staff. It was carnage!

Towards the end of hostilities there had been an instruction to put our guns down. I didn't hear it and shot Hales in the back of the leg.

My 'punishment' was to have to run down a hill and back up again, while everyone else could fire at me.

I must have been hit 100 times. You could play dot-to-dot on my body, there were red marks everywhere.

For days afterwards I was sore. For some reason everyone else seemed to find it funny though!

40

Coach Pick

I'VE KNOWN Andy Pick for almost as long as I've been playing cricket and every day has been a joy. The former Nottinghamshire seamer first worked with me during my time with the England under-19s and then as my bowling coach at Notts for many years.

We became good mates and if ever I needed to talk to anybody about anything Picky would be there for me.

Much of every summer would be spent with him and nothing would ever be too much trouble.

On home T20 matchdays I liked to have a bit of a bowl on the morning of a game, so we'd both go in around 10am and spend a good half an hour just nailing my yorkers.

One summer things were going pretty well for me with the ball and there was a little bit of newspaper talk about me perhaps getting an England call-up for T20s. Nothing ever came of it but I would have loved that, not just for myself but also as a way of Picky's work being recognised.

I know he feels I was capable of taking the next step up in my career.

* * *

Andy Pick: 'The first thing to tell you about Fletch is how dedicated he is with his practice sessions. But he needs challenges, he's not the sort of person who can just run in and bowl in practice.

'He needs targets setting for him, or maybe even a small wager, a pint on the side or something like that. How many times can he hit this target or that target? Be it eight times out of 12 or whatever, he needs to be challenged.

'That gets him going and is the secret of his success. He is driven to achieve and once he gets his teeth into something he won't let go.

'Even if he is going to come up short, he'll refuse to be beaten and will want to start again until he's hit whatever the particular target may be.

'I've never had to worry about his natural bowling length. He's a little bit like Kevin Cooper, who I used to play with, in that he can just rock up and hit the top of off four times out of six, without any preparation.

'For most people, move off that natural length and ask them to bowl yorkers or bumpers and it becomes more of a problem. But that's when Fletch excels.

'He gets his teeth stuck into something and he won't let go until he's mastered it.

'The question has always been about how driven he is. Where could his career have taken him? Who knows?

'He's certainly very talented, there's no doubt about that. Has he capitalised on it fully? Only he probably knows the answer to that one.

'Fletch might have missed the boat now in terms of further recognition but there was a period when the likes of Flintoff were talking up his talent all the time on television. That's sometimes the hard bit, getting yourself noticed and having done that there might have been a chance for him to get on the T20 bandwagon.

'But he's never been a hard-nosed mercenary and continually playing all around the world isn't for everyone.

'Perhaps he's not been looking for a bigger, better, flashier lifestyle, he's happy as he is and there's nothing wrong with that.

'He's certainly got a talent and probably still doesn't know how good he is or maybe how good he still could be.'

41

A Trip To Holland

UP UNTIL the last few seasons, when it all became regionalised, there used to be a random draw to decide the groups for the domestic one-day competition.

Ireland, Scotland, the Netherlands and the Unicorns, a side made up of several ex-first-class cricketers, Minor Counties stars and young hopefuls, were drawn into each of the four groups, alongside the 18 counties.

While Notts had trips to Dublin, Edinburgh and Wormsley (home venue for the Unicorns) to enjoy during my first few years at the club, I would often hear tales on the county circuit of how good the hospitality was in places like Amsterdam and Rotterdam.

Yorkshire had been two or three times and had taken the ferry over. High-jinx on the high seas by all accounts!

The draw for the 2013 Yorkshire Bank 40 competition was therefore greeted with more than a little excitement when we were paired with our Dutch friends.

For many months the venue for our clash remained a secret. On all fixture lists it was showing as TBA. I think we were all hoping for a little bit of downtime in Amsterdam.

Then it was announced. We would be playing the away match in the famous Dutch city of Truro.

Yes, Truro in Cornwall.

For reasons that I've never been entirely sure of, a link-up between the respective cricket associations of the Netherlands and of Cornwall had been forged through a mutual friendship.

So, instead of hopping on a plane at East Midlands Airport and being there in under an hour, we had to drive down.

If you've never done the journey from Nottingham to Truro by car it can be assessed as this: you drive all day and then you are about halfway there.

What made it worse for me was driving all that way and knowing that I wasn't going to be playing. The side hadn't been announced but I hadn't featured in the previous three or four one-dayers so I was expecting to be carrying the drinks again.

During warm-ups we were throwing a soft foam missile, called a Nerf Ball, around to each other and Jake Ball complained of a twinge in his back.

I was thrust into the starting XI and was straight out there after the Netherlands opted to bat first.

The Truro club couldn't have been any more welcoming. They'd gone into overdrive to make it a special day for everyone – everyone except the quicker bowlers, that is. It was a really tacky wicket and the ball just wouldn't zip through at all.

My opening spell was appropriately brief and by the time I came back on Readie was standing up to the stumps to everyone.

I decided to try a few off-cutters and surprised myself by how much assistance I was getting. Imagine then the shock on Tom Cooper's face when I bowled him.

Australian Tom, who played plenty of county cricket for Somerset, was guesting for the Dutch due to some fandangled regulation or other.

I sent an off-cutter down to him, on something like a fifth stump line. It gripped, turned sharply and came back to flatten his middle stump.

It's fair to say I've not picked up many wickets like that over the years but that was one of only a few memories from the day.

Most of our side were in on the joke of sending Samit Patel out to field on the boundary, right in front of the pork and stuffing van. There were long queues and a brisk trade there all day long but I'm sure they'd have all been knocked over in the rush if Samit had taken a couple of quid out on the field with him.

One man who did nip across there and tuck in during the interval was Ed Cowan. Our own Aussie was playing his final game for Notts before heading off to join up with his countrymen ahead of the forthcoming Ashes series.

Netherlands made 188/7 from their 40 overs and I sat back ready for some Alex Hales fireworks.

Our opener had been going through a bit of a lean run but looked in good form in the nets. I fancied him to put on a show for the large gathering.

Drilling his third ball straight to mid-off wasn't what I was expecting and, judging by his reaction, nor was he.

As angry as I've seen him, Hales kicked off a boot in frustration. I wasn't there when Sir Alex reputedly did something similar to David Beckham but I can now imagine the scene.

Hales's boot narrowly missed the head of teammate Sam Wood and made a hole in a wooden partition between the changing areas. Embarrassed, the culprit tried to cover up his actions by sticking a poster over the hole but somebody had snitched and Mick Newell came down on him like a ton of bricks.

There followed a fair amount of apologising to the home club.

James Taylor led us to victory with an unbeaten 90 and that was it, back on the road at the end of our Dutch adventure.

42

The Dublin Rain Card

A YEAR or two before the Truro adventure, we went to Dublin for a one-day match against Ireland. It was the first time I'd flown across the Irish Sea and I couldn't wait to see if the social side of things were as good as had been reported.

We went to the Clontarf ground a day early and it had been raining very heavily, making the outfield extremely wet. The forecast was pretty horrendous as well and none of us could see the possibility of any play, so we weighed up our options and decided to head out into town.

I wonder if you are familiar with the term 'rain card', used by cricketers when they know there's absolutely no chance of any play the next day.

We were spending just one evening in the Emerald Isle and our own eyes had told us that the chances of any cricket were slimmer than slim.

It turned into quite a night, as we toured the city and played the rain card pretty hard. Drinking Guinness in Dublin was a new experience for me – and it's one that I thoroughly approve of!

Drawing back the curtains next morning was a revelation in itself. We'd got it wrong. The skies had cleared and there was talk of a delayed start.

Full respect to the ground staff, who had worked extremely hard and managed to get the ground dry enough for a shortened game.

There were a few dusty heads as we took the field and the match turned out to be a lot closer than it should have been.

Ireland made 140/8 from a reduced allocation of 34 overs, with Samit taking career-best figures of 6-13.

We made hard work of it before scraping over the line by two wickets, with one ball remaining, with me at the crease as Paul Franks hit the winning runs.

43

Dan The Man

DAN CHRISTIAN is a really good bloke. I've neglected to mention him much so far but that needs addressing because he has become part of the Trent Bridge furniture over the past few years.

A no-nonsense Australian, he has perhaps been a little unlucky to have only played for his country in white-ball cricket but he has shown himself to be one of the leading all-rounders in the world and we've been extremely fortunate to have him at Notts.

He has led our T20 side magnificently over the years, getting us through to three Finals Days under his command, including our victory in 2017.

On one occasion, in the middle of our winter, I was speaking at a charity function in Beverly, Yorkshire.

Taking questions from the audience, I was put on the back foot by one lad's request, 'Could you FaceTime the most famous person in your phone book and ask them to donate

£100 to our foundation and if they don't, then you have to pay £200?'

You can't say no, can you?

So, with the full glare of the audience upon me I tried number after number, trying Stuart Broad, Graeme Swann, Alex Hales and Marcus Trescothick but none of them answered.

Then I tried Dan. He was fast asleep in bed in Melbourne and answered. I told him what it was about and immediately he agreed, before adding, 'Now can I go back to sleep?'

Top bloke!

44

Dancing On Ice

ENJOYING YOUR successes is one of the basics of sport and I'm delighted to have been involved in bringing some silverware back to Notts.

I did miss out on one fabulous occasion though, after the title win in 2010. It has become customary for the County Champions to be invited to Buckingham Palace to formally receive their medals.

That year, unfortunately, I'd already left the country to go and spend the winter playing in Australia.

I have been around to share our white-ball victories with the Nottingham public though and enjoyed going to the Ice Stadium to drop the puck ahead of a Panthers ice hockey game.

Managing not to fall, I somehow made it out to the middle of the stadium in my trainers, tottering about like a new-born giraffe. If the producers of *Dancing On Ice* were present, I won't be expecting a call any time soon.

More to my liking, in 2017 after the two white-ball successes we all went to Meadow Lane for a pre-season friendly between Notts County and Nottingham Forest and received a great ovation from the sporting public of the city while doing a lap of honour on the pitch.

45

Big Merv

A HOT day, a few beers and a round of golf. Nothing better to get you in the mood to meet an Australian cricket hero.

* * *

Chris Rattle: 'During Fletch's last stint with Buckley Ridges, the club had its annual golf day, always one of the most anticipated and fun days on our social calendar.

'Fletch had a great time on the course and worked his way through as many cans of beer as he could.

'That evening, for the gala dinner, we had Merv Hughes as our guest speaker and he told the legendary story of how David Boon had broken all known drinking records by downing 52 cans of beer on the Qantas flight from Sydney to London on his way across for the 1989 Ashes.

'Merv relayed to the audience how all the rest of the team had taken it in turns to drink with Boony, so the burly Tasmanian always had a drinking partner.

'Afterwards it was time for big Fletch to meet Big Merv and Nottinghamshire's gentle giant let it be known that he could smash that record – easily – and didn't need any drinking partners to help him either!'

46

Cashmere Calamity

WHO DOESN'T love a staff Christmas party? One year it was held in one of the local bars, the Monkey Tree in West Bridgford, and I was soon out of favour.

* * *

Notts press officer Michael Temple: 'Fletch had a couple of quick ones to get him started and then his table won a bottle of champagne as we played a game after the first course.

'He asked me what would happen if he did a Lewis Hamilton with it [spraying it about like a Grand Prix winner]. There were about 70 people there so it was calmly suggested that it might not be the best idea he'd ever had and probably wouldn't go down very well.

'Around ten minutes later he obviously couldn't resist the demons inside his head any longer. He stood up, yelled "Lewis Hamilton" and popped the cork.

'He certainly knows how to make an impression.

'The chief exec's new cashmere jumper was right in the line of fire and took the full force. Not for the first time, a red-faced Fletch had some apologising to do!'

* * *

It also meant an awkward start to the New Year when I bumped into the chief exec. I considered asking if the jumper had dried out by then but thought better of it.

Christmas parties have often been my downfall. The free bar sends me over the edge too easily and the rest of the lads know it. There's a reason I don't drink red wine, yet it didn't stop Chris Read from repeatedly filling my glass up at every opportunity one year.

I seem to recall, hazily, that led to an early evacuation from the Larwood and Voce after a few choruses of 'Charlie Shreck's barmy army!'

There was a plan that evening to make it to Hooters for chicken wings but after falling off a bar stool in The Globe I gave it a miss.

Christmas party? Bring it on!

47

The Fletch XI

AS WITH most cricketers, especially those who have been around for a while, I sometimes get asked about those I've played with and against and who I think the best were.

It's tough to do it because this is an era of outstanding cricketers and it's often very hard to judge one against another. There's no doubt that I'll be leaving out some outstanding players here and spoiling a few friendships but let's have a go anyway.

These are among the best I've played with and are a mixture of four-day, one-day and T20 players.

1 Hashim Amla

Hashim was ranked as the number one Test batsman in the world when he joined us at Nottinghamshire in 2010.

We won the title that year and it's worth noting that he played in four championship matches and we won all four, with him contributing 377 runs at an average of 75.40.

That's the sort of impact you hope your overseas signing will make. When he first arrived at the club I started to make up a song about him but it was very much a work in progress and was far from finished.

We headed up to Durham University and put out a strong side there, as it was only a week before the start of the new championship season.

Hashim was making his debut and in the team huddle beforehand Mick Newell caught me off guard and totally dropped me in it by telling Hashim that I'd got a song for him. Hash was looking straight at me and one or two others were urging me to sing it, so I started:

'Hashim, Hashim Amla
He's got a beard, like santa
He hits the ball through midwicket
He was born to play Test match cricket
Oh Hashim, Hashim Amla
His favourite food is veggie lasagne'

That was as far as I got before the others burst into laughter, but thankfully Hashim saw the funny side. We've always got on great over the years since and every time I see him he asks me to sing it for him. I must finish it one day!

I've played against Hashim a few times and he's an incredibly difficult man to bowl to. He's played for a few other counties and I remember him coming to Trent Bridge with Hampshire and scoring a very stylish hundred. He was so good.

He's a great man as well so walks into my side at the top of the order.

2 Alex Hales

He had to be in, didn't he? Hales and I are best mates and we've been through a lot of ups and probably even more downs together, so I have to include him.

As you'll have read earlier, we trialled together and even back in those days you could tell that this lad was a bit of a freak.

He would rock up in his Punto, with drum and bass music banging out from the back and would go out to bat in his school socks. He'd use his dad's 3lb Gray-Nicolls bat, which had four nails hammered in the bottom because it was knackered, then go out and blast a double hundred before tea. He was that good, honestly.

Looking at him then (or now) you wouldn't have thought that this bloke is a cricketer because he would turn up 20 minutes late for games armed with a McDonald's breakfast, he'd strap the pads on and smack a hundred. He was unbelievable.

He's one of those people that you sometimes get really excited about when he's not scoring runs because you sense he'll go on and do something crazy just around the corner.

Far too good to fail for very long, the bloke smacked 171 for England in an ODI and was the first to get a hundred in a

T20 international, then got 187 not out for Notts in a Lord's final. He does insane stuff.

3 James Taylor

Titch was one of the toughest lads for anyone to bowl at because he could really belt the ball for such a short man. I saw him score a couple of hundreds for us in one-day matches that were just incredible.

Apart from being such a class batsman, he was an unbelievable fielder as well. If he hadn't been forced into early retirement then I'm sure he would have gone on to do outstanding things for England and be a really top player in events like the IPL.

He had the ability to hit the ball all around the field, a proper 360 degrees player, and he was rapid between the wickets, a really important asset to have these days.

4 David Hussey

Next up is a Nottinghamshire club legend. Coming into the Notts set-up when I did, I was already in awe of Huss having always made a point of going down to Trent Bridge to watch him in the Friday night T20s.

Huss averaged something like 53 throughout his first-class career and yet didn't play a single Test match for Australia, which is outrageous. A great bloke, he was a top man to have in the dressing room and I've loved catching up with him whenever I've been over to Melbourne.

Now making his way as a successful coach in his homeland, he's also been used as a mentor for sides in the IPL. That's the sort of role that he'd be perfect at, someone who's been there and done it as a player and is now in a position to pass on all that experience.

5 Samit Patel

What a man Samit is. The stat I love most about him is that he's always had a bit of stick around his levels of fitness, yet he has never missed a match in his career through injury.

Admittedly, he's not James Taylor-esque between the wickets but he doesn't miss games of cricket and he's a proven matchwinner.

So many times over the years he's come good on the big occasion and delivered when it has most been needed. The times he does that on the big stage is ridiculous and it's pretty much accepted in our dressing room that if we're going to be live on Sky, then Samit will take the man of the match award.

Fitness is a strange thing, isn't it? If you define fitness I guess it's being able to do your job – in this case cricket – consistently well over a long period. Samit has produced runs and wickets throughout his career.

Give him a couple of Kit Kat Chunkys and a bag of Quavers and away he'll go.

Mind you, he does have his kryptonite. He doesn't like water, it's his Achilles' heel.

One pre-season we went whitewater rafting, which is pretty scary at the best of times. There's an element of danger and the water is flowing rapidly. But we had instructors there watching us and helping us and it was a pretty fun day all round.

Towards the end of the session they let us know we were going to be tipped in at some point, as we made our way down the course.

They explicitly told us what was going to happen. 'Accept it, lift your legs high and allow the current to take you down to the bottom.' It was like a giant wet slide effectively.

I was in a group with Samit and Harry Gurney.

Gurney and I did as we were told, were tipped in and away we went down to the bottom.

There, we heard a painful squealing noise coming from further up, 'Somebody help me, help me.'

In the middle of the course was a small tree and Samit was holding on to a few branches wailing pitifully.

He looked like a stranded whale. 'Help me!'

I couldn't help myself. You know when you are nearly sick because you are laughing so hard? That was me. I still chuckle now whenever I think of him being stranded there.

He said that if we ever get asked to do that again he'd rather donate £1,000 to the team's charity pot than be made to do it again.

Samit has been on the wrong end of a lot of stick over the years but he's been an absolute joy to play alongside.

Whether it's been with bat or ball we've all lost count of the number of games he's won for us and I think he's been a little unlucky not to have represented England far more than he did.

Despite the number of laughs I've sometimes had at his expense, thankfully there's never been any lasting damage to our wonderful friendship!

* * *

Samit Patel: 'Fletch has been a magnificent teammate over the years and one of the very best people to have in your dressing room.

'You could have had the s******t day imaginable yet he would still have the ability to make everyone laugh.

'I was in the team before him and can remember him coming along. No one tried to change him and that's right because he's become one of the most consistent line and length bowlers in the game. He thrives on keeping his economy level low and hates going for runs.

'He knows he's not blessed with the greatest of pace but his skill level is incredible and you need people like him because whatever the situation you find yourself in, he'll always come charging in for you.

'Fletch has become the "People's Man" because the crowd love him and he enjoys interacting with them.

'He's always given absolutely 100 per cent in whatever he's done and what he's achieved in the game I think is a great testament to him.'

6 Riki Wessels

Riki did some freakishly good things when he was at Notts, through all three formats of the game.

I remember him getting a double hundred in just two sessions against Sussex, doing crazy things like slog-sweeping Jofra Archer into the stands and stuff.

A little bit of an introvert, he didn't offer an enormous lot in the dressing room but he was a good man and would do anything for you, without question.

As a batter he was tough and would get pinned all the time because he liked sweeping seamers, so he'd always get struck on the fingers but he'd keep going and get stuck in.

When I was out of the side with my head injury I was asked to help the Radio Nottingham guys out on commentary for a few T20 matches and it was a real privilege to be on air when Riki hit a century against Derbyshire because I knew how much it meant to him.

When you consider some of the players I've not included in this list, you know how highly I rate him.

7 Chris Read (captain and wicketkeeper)

Readie could catch balls in his sleep, he was that good. I think in ten years he only dropped two off my bowling and one of those was really difficult, going right across first slip to try and get a glove on it.

People have said that he should have played more Test matches for England than he did and I have to agree.

There's no doubt that by the end of his career, 16,000 first-class runs, with 26 centuries at an average of over 37, he had the figures to back up those claims but he was possibly still improving as a batsman when he was in the national side.

His best days for Notts would always come when the side was in trouble and time after time he would dig us out of a hole. He probably realised that he had to contribute though, as it was unlikely that Fletcher would offer much after him!

No one could set a better example as he was one of the hardest trainers and one of the fittest blokes in the team and would go through all his drills every single day.

Out there with the gloves, he'd practise all his wicketkeeping skills, then he'd be off for a hit, always looking to improve. Non-stop, Readie was a class act and another really nice guy.

Some wicketkeepers like a lot of chatter behind the stumps but that wasn't Chris. He hardly said anything and I didn't hear him sledge anyone ever.

A lot of people who chirp all the time are pretty s**t anyway, aren't they? Chris didn't have to say anything, he was that good. Everyone knew it and he was respected throughout county cricket.

As a captain, he was remarkably calm and never really got flustered or resorted to shouting. That wasn't his nature, as he's such a quiet bloke really.

I held him in such high esteem, so when I came into the side, whatever he said I'd just do it. This was Chris Read for God's sake, a legend.

I'm so glad that we won the Lord's final in 2017 because that was his last big match and it provided a fitting send-off for him.

8 Graeme Swann

What a bonkers, crazy bloke Swanny is. I think, probably through his appearances on *Strictly Come Dancing,* more than his cricket, most folks have a good idea what it might be like sharing a dressing room with Graeme Swann.

There's no doubt, he was full-on to be around and could be quite scary, so you had to have a bit about you.

He's so quick-witted and constantly at it all day, so I could understand when people would keep their distance from him.

Me? I loved it. It was constant banter, so I would go out of my way to be around him. He was away with England a lot but I loved it when he was back with us because I loved the craic.

My championship debut was against Lancashire at Old Trafford and I roomed with Swanny that week and travelled up there and back with him.

He was quality.

Anyway, I managed to get a couple of wickets during the match, one of which was Faf du Plessis.

Swanny was clearly pleased for me and promised to treat me at the end of the match. On the way home we stopped off and he bought me the biggest Burger King meal imaginable and then took me for a pick 'n' mix.

I thought county cricket was great then. Get a couple of wickets and Test players will buy you Whopper meals.

I should also mention that he was an outstanding spin bowler and knew how to hold the bat as well.

9 Stuart Broad

I'm always getting asked what sort of bloke Broady is because everyone sees him as some kind of huge celebrity.

When you've known someone as a mate for years – we joined the Notts dressing room at the same time – I guess I only see him for what he is: a top, top lad, who couldn't be any more down to earth if he tried.

He is England's second best bowler of all time, statistically, yet he's just Broady to his county teammates.

Normally, he will be around us at the start of the county season, getting prepared for the international summer that follows. I find him particularly useful then, because he often dishes out bits of his spare Adidas kit to me – somehow, he always seems to have loads!

Spend any time with him at all and you'd know why he has been so successful. He is competitive at everything he does and absolutely loves winning, so whatever drills or warm-up routines we are doing, you want Broady on your side.

I'm not the slightest bit surprised that he has had the length of international career that he has because he is constantly striving to get better. He's always working on different things with his action, working on different balls, leg-cutters, off-cutters, anything that might give him an advantage because he has to play all over the world in the most trying of conditions.

As I said, we've become great mates, but that doesn't stop him from telling a few stories at my expense.

* * *

Stuart Broad: 'Fletch is the friendliest man in cricket and I've never seen him in any sort of conflict. In fact he's the one that always defuses tension out there. There was a day though, when I thought he was going to kick off at a respected opponent.

'Playing at Derby he took a wicket and that brought Shivnarine Chanderpaul to the crease.

'After delivering a ball he had a longer than normal follow-through. I thought, "He's not going to sledge him here, is he?"

'He went down and said to the great West Indian batsman, "Hello Mr C, it's an honour to be on the same field as you."

'Shiv just didn't know what to say!'

* * *

For some reason, Mr Broad always used to find amusement in my choice of going-out clothes:

'Fletch used to make sure he'd have his two favourite Hugo Boss polo shirts with him for away trips and we knew it was almost a code.

'If he'd got his orange one on then it was more than likely he planned to settle in the hotel bar or maybe just pop out for a quick Nando's or something like that.

'But if it was the black one! Then in all probability the night would be ended with a 2am kebab, it was his equivalent of Mickey Flanagan's "out out!"

'Nowadays, perhaps the most obvious sign of him growing up and being a little more responsible is that you'll usually find him in a Notts tracksuit throughout away trips.

'A sociable lime and soda in the hotel seems to be as far as he gets nowadays.

'Fletch appreciates everything about the life he's got and you are reminded of that virtually every morning.

'He'll just go and get a drink and tell everyone how lucky they are to be playing at Trent Bridge and he's right.

'Whether he's been given a cup of tea or a bacon sarnie he'll be grateful and can bring anyone down to earth over such simple things. He's the best teammate you could have, one of life's energy-givers!'

* * *

10 James Pattinson

I loved playing cricket with Patto, who must be up there among the very best I've played alongside, in terms of what he offers to the game.

He's my type of bloke. You put us together and we're the same character, although he's a lot better cricketer than me, unfortunately. He's far more professional than me because he has a strict off-field regime, being a firm believer in the benefits of pilates and daily stretching.

What I like most is the way he gets stuck in on the field, he loves a challenge and loves a fight. Players like him have an edge, they just want to win.

His brother Darren was made of the same stuff when he was at Notts but even he wasn't able to blow sides away like James did in his first spell with us.

In 2017 he took 32 wickets in only five championship matches, each of them costing only 12 runs, a phenomenal impact for a new arrival to make.

He was born in Australia but his family hail from Grimsby and there must be something about the Lincolnshire sea air in his genes because he absolutely loves his fish and chips when he's over here.

As well as being one of the quickest bowlers on the planet, he's a very decent left-handed bat and scored the winning runs for us in a Lord's final.

11 Andre Adams

Number 11 on this list but number one in my estimation. The former New Zealand international was far and away the best bowler I've played with. Dre was phenomenally good.

He was never keen on bowling with the new ball, so when he was at Notts my job was just to take it until he fancied a bowl.

If I hadn't got a wicket in my first three or four overs then that might be it for me, down to long leg to watch him work his magic and pick up a six-fer or a seven-fer.

Dre liked the ball to be around nine or ten overs old when he came on because he reckoned he could grip it better then.

What he did so well was hit a full length with such intensity that he'd get the ball just to nip off the wicket and he had such supreme control that he could wobble it either way. An absolute nightmare for batsmen to face, in his pomp he was the best around by a country mile.

Dre loved bowling at left-handers in particular. He used to start laughing when they came in and would go around the wicket straight away and normally would see them off quickly.

A better bat than he ever claimed to be, Dre had such a good eye and could hit the ball for many a mile. I used to hate batting behind him because I was always on the edge of my chair. You knew he would go hard at the bowlers but just didn't know if he'd sky the first ball straight up or would flog it around for half an hour.

Nottinghamshire's player of the season when we won the County Championship in 2010.

* * *

That's it, a side strong enough to give anyone a game, I fancy. The trouble with doing lists like these is that you are full of remorse about those you've left out and try and make a case for their inclusion.

One of those that would have been in was Andre Russell, the West Indies all-rounder. He was a proper superstar – he could bowl at 90mph, whack it around and was a gun fielder as well.

On checking, I decided he wasn't eligible for this list as we hadn't taken the field together. He joined Notts for part of the T20 campaign in 2016 but rain completely washed away three of the matches he was due to play in, so we were never out there on the pitch at the same time.

Russell apart, I could easily make a case for several other cricketers – in some cases very good friends – to be included.

Steven Mullaney would have to be the 12th man, someone who has given everything for Notts over the last decade in all three competitions.

And I could so easily have justified a place for such players as Mark Ealham, Peter Siddle, Ryan Sidebottom, Michael Lumb, Ali Brown, Dan Christian, Cheteshwar Pujara, Ravi Ashwin, Imran Tahir, Vernon Philander, Harry Gurney and Jake Ball. Not easy, is it?

48

Favourite Foes

I CONSIDER myself to be extremely fortunate to have played against some of the very best of my generation and this list could easily have contained the likes of Marcus Trescothick, Faf du Plessis, Glenn Maxwell, Shivnarine Chanderpaul or several others, all who have gone on to much bigger and better things since coming up against this lad from Bulwell.

You will recognise all of the names here. They will include your cricketing heroes – I know that because most of them are my cricketing heroes, also.

The fact that I've managed to get a few of them out as well brings a warm glow.

Here's a selection of the very best players I've faced:

1 Sir Alastair Cook

At the top of my order I must choose England's all-time leading run-scorer, someone who has been among the very best of his generation.

Sir Alastair is a terrific accumulator of runs and a difficult man to bowl at but I have taken his wicket in a competitive match, oh yes!

Thankfully, due to his England commitments, I haven't had to bowl at him too often but I did get him out in a one-day match at Chelmsford.

Admittedly, he did have a huge slog across the line – and he had scored 96 at the time – but I did bowl him and it's there on the scorecard: A.N. Cook bowled L.J. Fletcher (let's forget about the 96 bit, eh?).

The last time I played against him I remembered something I'd heard but dismissed as being nonsense.

Cook had been batting for about an hour and a half and making us look pretty ordinary, so I went up to him at a break and said, 'Is it true you don't sweat?'

He pulled off one of his batting gloves and gave it to me. I slipped it on and it was bone dry inside. Weird. On the very rare occasions that I bat for about five overs I have to call for a change of gloves, as they're usually saturated by then.

2 Rahul Dravid

Known as 'The Wall', Rahul Dravid was always one of my favourite players and it was a real privilege to get to play against him in our champion county match in Abu Dhabi in 2011.

At the time he was ranked among the very best in world cricket, with possibly only Sachin Tendulkar and Hashim Amla also vying for top spot.

I admit to having a few nerves as I ran in to bowl to the great man but those feelings soon evaporated as I thudded my second delivery into his pads.

Up went the umpire's finger. Got him. Out for a second-ball duck.

Dravid showed his mettle by scoring a brilliant century in the second innings, so I came away from that match feeling I'd got the very best of both experiences; picking up his wicket and then seeing at first hand just how brilliant the Indian Test star was.

We played a second match against MCC on that tour and our opponents swapped one Indian superstar for another.

Replacing Dravid was Sourav Ganguly, aka 'The Prince of Calcutta', but I was denied the opportunity of bowling at him, with Paul Franks getting him first ball, hit wicket!

3 Kane Williamson (captain)

I knew from the very first time I saw him play, that Kane Williamson was going to be a star. A thousand years ago when I played for England under-19s, he was captain of the New Zealand side against us and he looked a million dollars even then.

Our paths didn't cross again until a County Championship match at Trent Bridge in 2013. He'd just flown in to join Yorkshire for a short stint and made his debut against us.

I'd just removed the left-handed Andrew Gale, so had to adjust my line and sent it down, at around a fifth stump line.

Williamson had a massive nibble at it and nicked it firmly to Samit at second slip. Got him!

Whether it was jet-lag or not I'll take it, one of the best players around, gone first ball.

I think he's been a terrific leader for New Zealand as well, so would make him skipper of this all-star team.

4 Joe Root

What a player Joe Root is! We were on the wrong end of a terrific knock from the England captain at Trent Bridge in 2019. I'd just flattened the stumps of Gary Ballance to bring Root to the crease.

Pumped up and ready for the battle I pounded in, cheered on by words of encouragement from my teammates. The first ball landed exactly where I wanted but it then fizzed back straight past me and down the ground for four.

Exactly the same thing happened from the next delivery.

'S**t,' I thought. 'This is going to be a long day.' And it was.

I've not spent much time in his company but feel like I know him pretty well, almost through osmosis. His brother Billy played at Notts for a while and we'd always hear the tales and follow his progress.

His mum and dad are good fun too and often came to our matches to support Billy. I'll always remember his dad being on our coach on the way back from winning the T20 at Edgbaston. Let's just say, he knows how to celebrate!

5 Kumar Sangakkara (wicketkeeper)

This brilliant Sri Lankan probably should have been in the team as one of the best I've played with. In 2015 I had a brief loan spell with Surrey, which was arranged just before a match at Northampton.

I drove straight there to meet the team and arrived early. Shortly afterwards Kumar arrived and for a while it was just the two of us.

In professional sport you get used to meeting all sorts of famous people and tend to just shrug it off as an everyday occurrence.

With Kumar, it was different, I was genuinely star-struck but he couldn't have been more welcoming and appeared to take a real interest in me, as we chatted for half an hour before the rest turned up.

He was such a nice down-to-earth chap but that didn't stop me having a snarl when he put down a catch off my bowling in my second match for Surrey, at Beckenham against Kent.

Daniel Bell-Drummond nicked me to slip but the chance went begging. I'd have loved to have seen that on a scorecard: caught Sangakkara bowled Fletcher!

Later that same year he scored a brilliant 166 in the one-day semi-final against us at The Oval, winning the match virtually on his own. That went a long way to explaining our reaction when Steven Mullaney got him cheaply in the final two years later.

6 Ben Stokes

What a summer Ben Stokes had in 2019, playing his part in the World Cup Final win with a brilliant innings of 84 not out to take the match to a Super Over.

Then he scored that brilliant Ashes century at Headingley, putting on an unbroken 76 for the last wicket with Jack Leach.

Throughout those epic performances I was happy to tell anyone who would listen a fact – something that I now discover to be a complete and utter lie.

For several years I have been under the misapprehension that Stokes made his debut for Durham in a one-day match against us. During that particular encounter in 2009 I clean-bowled the young, ginger-haired lad for not very many.

'I was the first to bowl Stokes out in county cricket, you know,' I would happily tell anyone who might come dangerously within earshot.

As it happens – checking facts for this book – Vikram Banerjee of Gloucestershire beat me to it, so I was second.

I've been out socially with Ben a time or two and he's cracking company, although that's not how I was describing him in the 2014 one-day semi-final when he scored a big hundred against us. We'd dropped him early on and were made to pay.

Every time I ran in to bowl he just belted me for four or six. Too good.

7 Andrew Flintoff

Although our respective careers overlapped slightly, I didn't get to play against one of my heroes until he made a brief comeback in 2014.

Watching the Ashes on television in 2005 helped convince me that I wanted to play cricket for a living, if I could. That series had absolutely everything and provided so many memories for so many people. It certainly went a long way to cementing my love affair with the sport.

Andrew 'Freddie' Flintoff was at the heart of it, of course, giving everything with both bat and ball. A hard but fair competitor, I felt that I could relate to him and his style of play, and I saw him as a similar kind of character to me.

I guess he was my first cricketing idol.

As I've mentioned elsewhere, he actually announced his retirement from the game on the day that we won the title at Old Trafford in 2010.

His body was letting him down constantly by then and he had stopped playing, although his hunger for the game certainly hadn't left him.

So, properly healed and rested, Freddie was tempted to make a comeback in 2014 after being given a chance to play for Lancashire in the T20 competition.

Understandably, he needed a little bit of match practice beforehand and made his return to the game in a second XI trophy match against Notts at Worksop College. Both sides had a smattering of first- and second-team players and it turned into a cracking match, with them eventually chasing down 270-odd.

I faced him for a few deliveries at the end of our innings and he could still find his yorkers. Understandably, his pace was down from his best years but he could still push it through at a decent lick.

Later, when he came out to bat he was facing Jake Ball. The first one was smacked back over Bally's head for a one-bounce four.

I thought, 'Here we go!' He nicked one from me through the slips and made 40 from only 23 balls before Brett Hutton bowled him.

We nattered for a while afterwards and I hope he sees a kindred spirit in me. Certainly, he remembered me because a few years later, completely out of the blue, he got in touch.

A private message appeared from Freddie, asking if I wanted to come and see him. He was appearing in Nottingham in the stage musical, *Fat Friends*.

Kirsty came with me and he'd left us tickets and backstage passes. He couldn't have been any nicer and it was an evening we'll both always remember.

However, I must at this point clear up something and state equivocally that our son Freddie is not named after the former England all-rounder. We both just love the name, honestly.

And our daughter Rosie isn't named after former Somerset captain Brian Rose either!

8 Simon Harmer

There have been personal anecdotes for most of the players in this hypothetical list but not this time. I don't think I've even spoken to Simon Harmer.

He makes this XI purely on skill alone. I think he's a tremendous cricketer and has managed to winkle me out quite easily on a number of occasions.

One of the reasons that Essex have picked up a number of domestic trophies in recent years is because the South African off-spinner has few equals in the county game.

9 Jeetan Patel

Alongside Harmer, I'd have to say that Jeetan Patel is one of the best spinners I've played against. He's another I could have included in my list of outstanding former teammates because I spent a winter playing alongside him with Wellington.

From those days I recall him being a generous host; he certainly showed me around the very best places to visit in his home city.

On the field he can be a fierce competitor but someone you'd rather have with you than against you. A class operator, he's given Warwickshire more than a decade of outstanding service.

10 Graham Onions

One year, in a match against Durham at Trent Bridge, I unwittingly spoiled things for their fabulous fast bowler Graham

Onions and became a nerdy pub quiz question at the same time.

Onions had been in an England squad of 12 or 13 but was then released on the morning of a Test and allowed to join a County Championship match at Trent Bridge that was already two days old.

'Bunny', as he's known, didn't take too long before making his mark, picking up wicket after wicket after wicket.

He is a magnificent bowler on his day and this was certainly his day, slicing his way through our batting card with consummate ease, taking all eight wickets as we slumped to 153/8.

I can only imagine (I can't really as I've never had more than five wickets in a first-class innings) what he was feeling at that stage, being on the brink of a ten-wicket haul.

At that stage he virtually had the ball on a string, wobbling it about at his beck and call.

Opportunities of taking all ten opposition wickets are extremely rare in any form of the game but his dream of making history were unceremoniously shattered by yours truly, who arrived at the crease and decided he wasn't prepared to loiter down at the danger end for very long.

Planning an innings has never been my greatest strength and this was no exception. Caught in the headlights, I decided to scamper an impossible run to get away from the strike but I'd hit the ball straight to Onions.

He had a dilemma. Throw the stumps down for a certain run-out or hang on to the ball and continue trying to get all ten?

I was run out by about 15 yards.

He immediately closed out our innings by clean-bowling Andy Carter for another duck. 'Bunny' had taken 9-67 and he still curses me to this very day about the wicket he didn't get!

11 James Anderson

England's leading Test match wicket-taker quite rightfully breezes into this list. Trent Bridge has always been one of his favourite hunting grounds and it won't surprise you to hear that I'm on his list of victims there.

One year I got him out though. First ball, he nicked a yorker through to Chris Read.

When I went in to bat he returned the favour. I didn't see it but fortunately nicked it down to fine leg for four. He glared at me. 'Bit quicker than yours, big lad? Yours came down with a bit of a dip in it.'

I never knew what to make of him on the cricket field and always thought he had a bit of white line fever out there.

Over the past few years I've started playing a bit of golf and am always happy to make up the numbers when asked. I've played a few times for Stuart Broad's team on his charity golf day against Jimmy Anderson's team and found the Lancashire man to be a really nice fella.

Though on one of those trips I got a bit lost, as Broady recalls: 'Fletch came along as part of my team when we had the chance for a charity golf match at Close Hall, near Newcastle.

'I got up a team of 12, which included friends and teammates and we were up against a side put together by Jimmy Anderson.

'All good fun and we just about had the place to ourselves for our two-day stay. We played golf on the first day, had a meal and a fines session and a few beers until around 1am when most people decided it was time to turn in. There were morning tee times to think about.

'Fletch and one or two others seemed keen on having a couple more, so I left them to it.

'At breakfast it quickly went round that something had occurred. It transpired that having had his extra couple of drinks Fletch not only couldn't find his way back to room 21, he couldn't find the right building.

'He must have missed the sign in front of the owner's house that said, "PLEASE RESPECT PRIVACY, PRIVATE HOUSE, KEEP OUT" and decided to ring the doorbell.

'And he rang it, and rang it, and rang it until eventually a private security firm came and escorted him back to the right building!'

12th man Kevin Pietersen

I should have found a place for Kevin Pietersen, who I've played against a time or two when he was at Surrey, so I'll put him on 12th man duty.

KP was another hero of mine from that 2005 Ashes series that had me glued to every ball.

It's a shame that he'd left Notts by the time I started, as I'd have loved to have been around him regularly and seen what made him tick, what made him an international cricketer.

The nearest I've ever got to England duty came when I was asked to do the 12th man chores at a couple of Trent Bridge Tests. Young reliable lads get asked to help out, take the drinks out, etc. – and on occasions do a bit of fielding.

One year, I think it was for the Pakistan Test match in 2010, I had carried the drinks out but not done a great deal else when I was asked to stay behind.

'Oh s**t, am I in trouble?' was the first thought that went through my head.

As it happens, it turned out to be something completely different, a real treat for me.

KP had been in the dressing room all day and fancied having a net. For almost an hour after everyone had gone home I ran in, bowling at him, working with him at the closest of quarters. I loved it, of course.

49

And Now...

THE 2019 season was certainly one to forget for all of us at Notts. We've enjoyed a few decent runs in the limited overs stuff during the last few years and another Lord's final was within our grasp until we ran into a strong Somerset side in the semi-final.

On the day we were no match for them and were easily beaten and it was no real surprise when Tom Abell's outfit went on to lift the trophy. Losing to the eventual winners is not really a consolation but I couldn't really argue that they weren't the best side around.

Our County Championship form was wretched – we hadn't tasted victory in that format since June 2018 and couldn't break that streak as we failed to move off the bottom of Division One at any point.

Relegation was an inevitable outcome, so our last and only hope of giving the supporters something to cheer about came with our progression to a third T20 Blast Finals Day in four years.

Back to Edgbaston we went, looking to regain the crown we'd won in 2017 and once again I was on the sidelines.

I was changed and part of the squad, ready to be called upon in the event of injury or emergency, but we'd had a settled team for the most part and I wasn't part of it.

While Essex and Derbyshire were paired together in the second semi-final, we had been drawn against defending champions Worcestershire Rapids in the day's opening match.

Matt Carter, brother of Andy, had enjoyed a terrific season for us and his three wickets helped to restrict the Rapids to only 147/9.

On the bench we were fairly confident as a group of chasing that down, although Worcestershire have had the knack of battling to a few unexpected wins over us in recent years.

This time it appeared to be our turn. Certainly there was only going to be one outcome as we motored to 100/1.

Then Baz got out. Then the turning point, because our run-rate started to drop alarmingly.

We were still in charge and only needed 11 runs from the final two overs but a calamitous period saw us slide from 137/2 to 140/5.

Time for cool heads. Samit joined Ben Duckett in the middle. Seven were required from the final over – to win. Hang on, we'd go through with a tie, having lost fewer wickets.

Do they know? Are they aware?

'Fletch, go and take some spare gloves out and tell them a tie will do us.'

The over ticked along like that.

I was repeatedly being sent out, with water, gloves, anything, just as a ruse to make sure they knew the situation.

Each time I went on the field my reception was less cordial. The crowd of 25,000 people were booing me and telling me to get off.

The gentle giant was a pantomime villain. 'Boo, get off.'

Even Bumble was talking to me through the audience at home. 'Get off Fletch, get off the field,' he was yelling in mock annoyance.

I was having a great day, left out and now being vilified in all quarters.

One run from the final ball would have given us a tie and a place in the final but Wayne Parnell bowled a terrific delivery, which Duckett missed, and that was it. We were out.

See ya later Birmingham. Tata folks.

You win as a squad and lose as a squad, so we were all pretty low at the outcome. Shell-shocked is probably a better word because you seldom lose matches, especially matches of that importance, from such a strong position.

But we had – and in many ways it summed up our entire season. Just not enough consistency, not enough quality and not enough players taking charge of the pressure moments.

A very definite line was drawn underneath the 2019 season at that point. One to forget for sure, although personally there was a boost when I was announced as the Nottinghamshire Player of the Year.

* * *

If you have followed cricket to any degree over the last two or three years then you would have been aware of the ECB's plans to introduce a new competition. Something totally original, totally fresh. New teams and a different format.

After much toing and froing the concept of The Hundred was evolved. A slightly shorter competition than the T20 Blast but something that could be nicely fitted into a three-hour time slot. Plans were also drawn up for the matches – or at least some of them – to be screened on terrestrial television.

Many of the world's leading players committed themselves and a start date of 2020 was confirmed.

The competition would take players away from their counties for a short spell, leaving those that remained behind to compete in a weakened one-day competition instead.

The idea of The Hundred appealed to me, as a cricket fan. I assumed I would be looking on from the outside but thought it would be exciting and fast-paced and would showcase some of the very best talent around. While I have confidence in my own ability, I am also a realist and could see that there was only so much jam to be spread around.

With only eight sides, selecting 14 or 15 players, there were going to be a lot of unlucky cricketers on draft night. There are also plenty within the game that are pigeon-holed as 'red-ball' players or haven't had much of a chance, for various reasons, with the white ball.

My career record in T20 isn't too bad but I was only picked for four of the Outlaws' matches in 2019, so it was only out of curiosity and support for some very good friends and teammates that I switched on to watch the coverage on Sunday, 20 October 2019.

We had been away at a wedding for the weekend and only came back at around the time the draft was starting. I sort of watched it early on and got more interested as it progressed, congratulating each of the Notts lads as they got selected, whether it was for the Trent Bridge-based franchise, Trent Rockets, or in the case of lads like Dan Christian, Joe Clarke and Ben Duckett, for other teams.

There was a strong contingent of home-based players being snapped up by Trent Rockets.

In pre-arranged picks they had already signed Baz Hales and Harry Gurney as 'local icon players', plus the England Test captain Joe Root, under the 'centrally contracted' banner.

Trent Rockets had the first overall pick when the draft started and immediately went with Rashid Khan of Afghanistan, before adding two Australians, D'Arcy Short and Nathan Coulter-Nile, as their other overseas options.

My Notts teammates Steven Mullaney, Matt Carter and wicketkeeper Tom Moores were also chosen, as was Luke Wood, who had recently announced a move away from Trent Bridge to join Lancs.

I congratulated them all and watched as players up and down the country – big names, decent professionals and young hopefuls gained contracts.

This competition is going to be a huge success, I thought.

The draft was drawing towards the close, down to the eighth round I think – players in the £30,000 category – when suddenly my name was announced.

I was absolutely shaken with disbelief. Kirsty started leaping around all excited, really pleased for me.

She thought I'd been having her on when I said I'd got no chance of being picked, having hardly featured in the Notts T20 side during the summer.

I thought there was no way I'd be picked up but here we were, at ten o'clock at night, dancing around the living room together.

To say I was shocked would be a massive understatement but the reality began to hit home as more and more well done messages kept pinging on my mobile.

One of the first was from my county captain, Steven Mullaney.

Steven Mullaney: 'Fletch was astonished to be picked. He genuinely didn't think anyone would take a punt on him and I'd heard him saying that he'd be playing the limited-overs stuff at Grantham when it was all going on.

'But I think he's a great pick and for the Trent Rockets to get Fletch and then Luke Wright in the £30,000 bracket was outstanding work but no one should be surprised.

'The day after we talked and I remember him saying he thought it was a dream. Hopefully whenever it all gets to happen he'll be able to have a crack at it.'

* * *

The following morning, wearing a ropy old Forest t-shirt and pants, I was tucking into a boiled egg when my phone rang.

It was a Face Time call from Kunal Manek, the Notts analyst who had been working on the draft.

Only it wasn't Kunal looking at me, as I tried to prevent yolk from dribbling down my chin. It was Stephen Fleming, the Trent Rockets head coach, my new gaffer.

'Morning,' he said. 'I just wanted to say congratulations and say how much I'm looking forward to working with you.'

I mumbled something that was probably inaudible in reply and with that he was gone. A brief moment in his day but a memorable one for me.

Trying to absorb what the selection may mean for me is difficult. The Hundred has been put back to at least 2021 because of the coronavirus pandemic and who knows what may happen even then?

I might just be a squad player, running on with drinks every now and again or I might get an opportunity to rub shoulders with the very best.

Either way, it's given me something really exciting to look forward to in the future, although it will never overshadow the pride I have had in playing for Nottinghamshire all these years.

Hopefully I've got a little bit more left in the tank and hopefully I'll get to spend it with some of the very best people I know. I've given one or two teammates a bit of stick in the previous chapters but I'm sure they'll all accept it in the way it has been intended.

Certainly, one fella has been mentioned as much as anyone in some of my escapades, so I ought to leave the final word to Alex Hales, as he reflects on our relationship.

Alex Hales: 'Fletch has mentioned meeting me for the first time, my recollection is of thinking that he was much older than he was at the time.

'Fitness clearly hadn't been a big thing in his life either, he was a big lad! I'd been playing for the MCC Young Cricketers and told him all about that in our first conversation.

'He seemed interested and asked me if I thought he would have a chance there, if things didn't work out with Notts.

'Inwardly I was thinking, "No chance pal, you're way too old!" But I did think he would make a good doorman.

'It didn't take long before I knew we were going to click. Straight away, I could tell he was a very likeable character and had a great sense of humour. I was drawn to him and knew we were going to be friends.

'When we started playing together for Notts seconds he would always get four or five wickets and I knew that he was going to carve out a successful career for himself.

'He was so accurate with the ball, always probing around the top of off stump. I used to stand in the slip cordon to him then, just waiting for the inevitable nick to come my way.

'There was always that feeling, the only other time I've had it was when I've been at slip for Andre Adams at Trent Bridge in April or May. He was that good.

'They always say, "You shouldn't live with your best friend." Well, we did and just about survived it with our friendship intact. I'm sure we learned a lot about each other – I know he thinks I was pretty messy to share with back then!

'We used to frequent the Toby Carvery for our Sunday roast and anywhere that there was an all-you-can-eat buffet for about six quid, we'd be on to it.

'Each Thursday was a big night out for us but the problem was we'd always be scheduled to have a gym session at 10am on the Friday. Most weeks we would go to that having only had about four or five hours of sleep. At that age I think we both thought we were super-heroes and could do it!

'Fletch is the most likeable bloke I've ever met and I always look forward to catching up with him for a chat.

'Whenever my phone rings and I see that it's him I start giggling straightaway because I know he'll have me in stitches for the next ten minutes.

'There can't be a better yorker bowler around, particularly in T20 cricket and no one was more delighted than me when Fletch was picked to play in The Hundred.

'We know that has now been delayed for a while but hopefully he'll still get his big chance and that could just be the start of the next chapter in his life.'

50

Stats

FIRST-CLASS CAREER RECORD 2008–2020

Nottinghamshire debut: 23 April 2008 v Oxford University Centre of Cricketing Excellence (The Parks, Oxford)

Highest scores:

92 Nottinghamshire v Hampshire (The Rose Bowl, Southampton, 2009)

92 Nottinghamshire v Durham (The Riverside, Chester-le-Street, 2017)

64 Nottinghamshire v Derbyshire (Trent Bridge, Nottingham, 2013)

58 Nottinghamshire v Somerset (County Ground, Taunton, 2013)

Best bowling:

5-27 Nottinghamshire v Worcestershire (New Road, Worcester, 2018)

5-50 Nottinghamshire v Essex (County Ground, Chelmsford, 2019)

5-52 Nottinghamshire v Warwickshire (Trent Bridge, Nottingham, 2013)

5-67 Nottinghamshire v Yorkshire (North Marine Road, Scarborough, 2019)

5-82 Nottinghamshire v Lancashire (Trent Bridge, Nottingham, 2011)

5-93 Nottinghamshire v Yorkshire (Trent Bridge, Nottingham, 2013)

First wicket – 23 Apr 2008 v Oxford University Centre of Cricketing Excellence (The Parks, Oxford) E. Abel, bowled

100th wicket – 8 April 2012 v Worcestershire (Trent Bridge, Nottingham) S.H. Choudhry, lbw

200th wicket – 17 Sep 2014 v Sussex (Trent Bridge, Nottingham) M.H. Yardy, caught S.R. Patel

300th wicket – 28 June 2018 v Worcestershire (Trent Bridge, Nottingham) D.Y. Pennington, caught M.H. Wessels

Surrey debut – 18 May 2015 v Northamptonshire (County Ground, Northampton)

Derbyshire debut – 17 April 2016 v Gloucestershire (County Ground, Bristol)

LIST A CAREER RECORD

Notts Outlaws debut – 4 May 2008 v Northamptonshire (Trent Bridge, Nottingham)

Highest scores:

53* Notts Outlaws v Kent (Trent Bridge, Nottingham, 2018)

46* Notts Outlaws v Lancashire (Trent Bridge, Nottingham, 2019)

Best bowling:

5-56 v Derbyshire (County Ground, Derby, 2019)

4-20 v Worcestershire (Trent Bridge, Nottingham, 2018)

4-44 v Warwickshire (Trent Bridge, Nottingham, 2014)

First wicket – 4 May 2008 v Northamptonshire (Trent Bridge, Nottingham) N. Boje, caught C.M.W. Read

50th wicket – 27 July 2016 v Yorkshire (North Marine Road, Scarborough) D.J. Willey, caught J. Ball

T20 CAREER RECORD

Notts Outlaws debut – 25 May 2009 v Durham (Trent Bridge, Nottingham)

First wicket – 25 May 2009 v Durham (Trent Bridge, Nottingham) P. Mustard, caught A.D. Hales

50th wicket – 15 May 2015 v Birmingham Bears (Trent Bridge, Nottingham) R. Clarke, bowled

Wellington Firebirds debut – 1 November 2014 v Northern Districts (Seddon Park, Hamilton)

Notts Outlaws v Surrey

	Royal London One-Day Cup 2017 (Final)
Venue:	Lord's Cricket Ground, St John's Wood on 1 July 2017 (50-over match)
Toss:	Surrey won the toss and decided to bat
Result:	Nottinghamshire won by 4 wickets
Umpires:	RT Robinson, AG Wharf
TV umpire:	DJ Millns
Scorers:	KR Booth (Surrey), R Marshall (Nottinghamshire)
Man of the Match:	AD Hales

Surrey innings		Runs	Balls	Mins	4s	6s	S-Rate
JJ Roy	c Mullaney b Patel	23	25	49	3	-	92.00
MD Stoneman	not out	144	149	210	12	-	96.64
KC Sangakkara	c Read b Mullaney	30	36	49	3	-	83.33
SG Borthwick	c Mullaney b Patel	14	20	22	1	-	70.00
+BT Foakes	b Mullaney	1	2	5	-	-	50.00
OJD Pope	c Mullaney b Patel	4	3	5	1	-	133.33
SM Curran	b Pattinson	24	31	35	2	-	77.42
TK Curran	run out (Patel)	16	18	18	1	-	88.89
*GJ Batty	b Fletcher	11	11	21	1	-	100.00
JW Dernbach	c Wessels b Gurney	5	6	9	-	-	83.33
R Rampaul	not out	0	0	2	-	-	0.00
Extras	(1b, 12lb, 2nb, 10w)	25					
Total	(9 wickets, 50 overs)	297					

Fall of wickets: 1-83 (Roy, 11.1 ov), 2-141 (Sangakkara, 22.5 ov), 3-172 (Borthwick, 29.6 ov), 4-175 (Foakes, 30.4 ov), 5-180 (Pope, 31.2 ov), 6-228 (SM Curran, 40.4 ov), 7-255 (TK Curran, 44.3 ov), 8-282 (Batty, 48.2 ov), 9-296 (Dernbach, 49.5 ov)

	O	*M*	*R*	*W*	*Wides*	*No-Balls*
Fletcher	5	0	37	1	1	-
Gurney	7	0	47	1	1	1
Pattinson	10	0	48	1	2	-
Patel	10	0	51	3	-	-
Broad	9	0	51	0	2	-
Mullaney	9	0	50	2	-	-

Nottinghamshire innings		Runs	Balls	Mins	4s	6s	S-Rate
MJ Lumb	lbw b SM Curran	4	9	17	-	-	44.44
AD Hales	not out	187	167	200	20	4	111.98
MH Wessels	lbw b Rampaul	6	9	21	1	-	66.67
SR Patel	c SM Curran b Rampaul	7	11	27	-	-	63.64
BRM Taylor	c Foakes b Dernbach	11	10	22	1	-	110.00
SJ Mullaney	lbw b SM Curran	5	17	20	-	-	29.41
*+CMW Read	c Stoneman b SM Curran	58	57	85	7	-	101.75
JL Pattinson	not out	9	9	10	1	-	100.00
SCJ Broad	did not bat						
LJ Fletcher	did not bat						
HF Gurney	did not bat						
Extras	(3lb, 4nb, 4w)	11					
Total	(6 wickets, 47.5 overs)	298					

Fall of wickets: 1-25 (Lumb, 3.5 ov), 2-60 (Wessels, 8.4 ov), 3-104 (Patel, 14.5 ov), 4-128 (Taylor, 19.4 ov), 5-150 (Mullaney, 25.1 ov), 6-287 (Read, 45.5 ov)

	O	*M*	*R*	*W*	*Wides*	*No-Balls*
Dernbach	10	0	53	1	-	-
SM Curran	9.5	0	68	3	2	-
TK Curran	6	0	52	0	1	1
Rampaul	10	0	52	2	1	1
Borthwick	3	0	29	0	-	-
Batty	9	0	41	0	-	-

Acknowledgements

WELL THAT'S it for now folks! There is no more, at least for the time being. I hope you've enjoyed reading *Tales from the Front Line* and getting to know me a little better.

Putting this book together has been a bit of an eye-opener for me and certainly wouldn't have happened but for the amazing contribution from so many people.

You'll have read lots of anecdotes from those that have helped me along my journey, from school-teachers, coaches, employers, teammates, umpires and friends and to each and every one of them – and the many others I've forgotten to mention – a heartfelt thank you.

I must give a special shout out to Mick Newell for believing in me in the first place and to everyone I've ever shared a dressing room with, only they can truly appreciate the bond we have formed and the experiences we have been through together.

Thanks too, to all the opponents who have appreciated the way I've chosen to enjoy my cricket and have become friends as a result.

In particular, I owe a huge debt of thanks to Freddie Flintoff, who kindly agreed to write a few words for me at the start of the book. He was an early hero of mine and getting to know him a little better over the years has been an absolute joy.

Closer to home, regular appeals for help from those at Trent Bridge have been greatly appreciated; particular thanks to Tom Holdcroft, Dan Robbins and Matt Freeman from the Notts CCC media team, as well as to Imogen Ward from The Hundred.

I hope you have enjoyed looking at some of the fabulous photographs we've included, so thanks to all involved in putting them together, particularly Simon Trafford, who provided the front cover photo and sourced many of the others and to David Griffin, for the Derbyshire photograph.

A big thank you to the fabulous team at Pitch Publishing for giving me this opportunity, especially Jane Camillin, Duncan Olner, Graham Hales, Alex Daley and Dean Rockett.

That just leaves me with enough space to thank Dave Bracegirdle for encouraging me to come forward and deliver my stories to a wider audience. Dave has been there with me, right from the start of my career, sharing in my successes and mourning my misfortunes.

There have been a lot of laughs and a few tears along the way and he's helped me record most of them in *Tales from the Front Line*.

Finally, a special thank you to my wonderful family. Mum, dad, Tom and Sam have always been so supportive and have always been there whenever I've needed them – and last of all, none of it would matter a great deal if I didn't have a loving partner and family to share it all with.

To Kirsty, Freddie and Rosie – I love you!

Thank you all, Fletch.

Photograph credits:

Front Cover Simon Trafford @TraffCricket

Photo Section One

Pages 1-4 all from Jane Fletcher's Private Collection

Page 5 Top and bottom right from Jane Fletcher's Private Collection, bottom left PA Images

Page 6 Top Getty Images, bottom Getty Images

Page 7 Top Luke Fletcher's Private Collection, bottom Dave Bracegirdle's Private Collection

Page 8 all from Buckley Ridges CC

Photo Section Two

Page 1 Top David Griffin, middle Getty Images, bottom Getty Images

Page 2 Top Left Getty Images, Top Right Getty Images, bottom Getty Images

Page 3 all Luke Fletcher's Private Collection, except bottom right Simon Trafford @TraffCricket

Page 4 top and bottom left Sky Sports, centre Getty Images, bottom right Jake Ball's Private Collection

Page 5 top and middle right Luke Fletcher's Private Collection, middle left Nottinghamshire County Cricket Club, bottom Getty Images

Page 6 top Getty Images, bottom Tony Marsh @Cricpix

Page 7 top PA Images, middle Dave Bracegirdle's Private Collection, bottom left and right Luke Fletcher's Private Collection

Page 8 top ECB, bottom Luke Fletcher's Private Collection

Back Cover Pro Sports Images

Also available at all good book stores

9781785316302

9781785316623

9781785315329

9781785316340

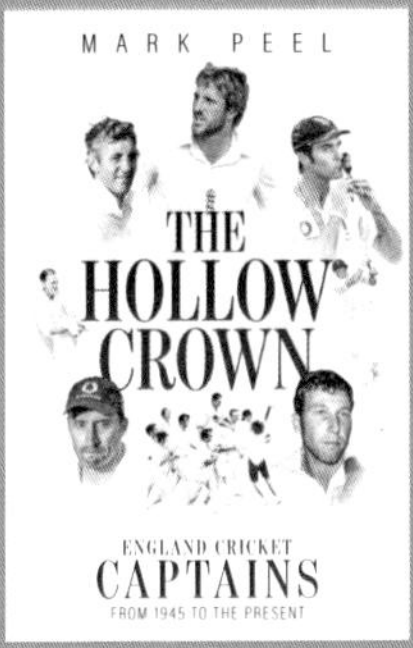

9781785316630

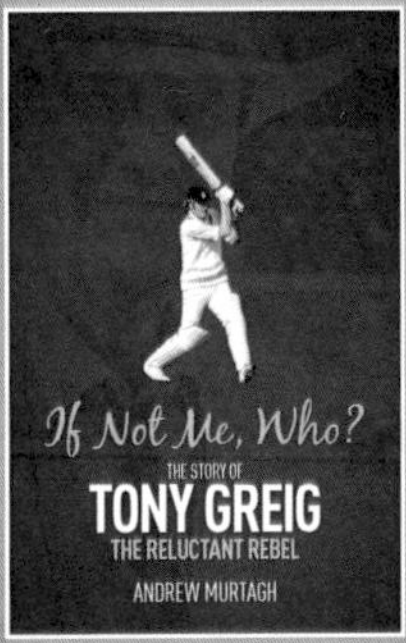

9781785316418

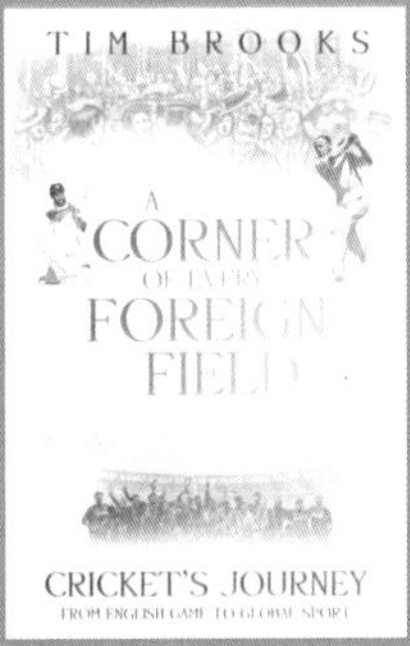

9781785316395

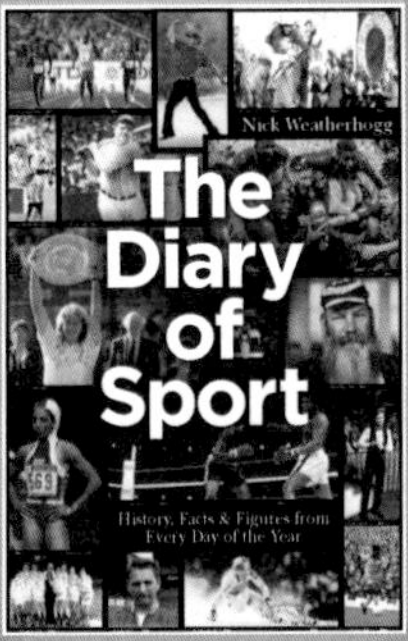

9781785316289

9781785316197